Pre-publication
DRAFT
Copy

Musings from 128 days

AROUND

THE

WORLD

Kyle Denning

For Mom

Who said the single week she spent on
a cruise ship was the most fun she ever had.

Contents

Preface

I've always thought a cruise around the world would be the perfect way to see it. A bit spendy, but far less expensive than every other mode of world travel, excepting possibly a global motorcycle ride. But my body clock has long since chucked that fantasy. The spirit is willing; the flesh is done.

Several years ago, I suggested a world cruise to Christeen. Her response was, "No way, I have a life. After three weeks on ship, I'd be bored out of my mind. Plus, I couldn't possibly be away from my grandbabies for that long!" Over the years, my continued subtle suggestions generated similar responses.

Then great grandchildren began to appear and an interesting, if somewhat unexpected, phenomenon emerged. Great grandma discovered that she was not the grandma. Our daughters were. And they did not want great grandma taking over their divine right to care for the new mommies and babies. In other words, stay out of the way, Mom.

The reality is great grandparents are preferably loved and adored from a distance. The kids are happy we're still alive and want us to check in from time to time. But take over? No way.

That realization, coupled with the fact that our youngest grandchild is nearly a teenager, and teenagers are entirely too distracted for doting grandparents, has released Christeen from her natural helicopter-granny instincts. Against her will, of course.

Which meant her sole remaining objection was the fear of depressing boredom on successive sea days. But our kids told her not to worry. Then over the holidays last year, she finally said she would do it. Right away, I reserved the Holland America Lines, 128-day World Cruise, departing Ft. Lauderdale, Florida on January 3, 2023.

Sleepless in Ft Lauderdale

Tuesday, January 3rd

Last fall, I debated using my Southwest Airlines frequent flier miles for flights to Ft Lauderdale, but because of the Covid pandemic, I decided booking through Holland America would be less risky. It was a wise choice. A few days before Christmas, Southwest's "Skysolver" flight control system imploded during a brutal winter storm, leaving flight crews and airplanes out of sync all across the country. By December 29th, more than 13,000 Southwest flights had been canceled, and the disruption continued over the New Years weekend. We were fortunate to have reserved American Airlines flights through Holland America.

With our bags pre-shipped on December 14th, the last item on our pre-embark checklist was negative Covid tests, required 24 hours before embarkation. On New Year's day, we took the prescribed, super accurate PCR tests at a local clinic. The clinic emailed the test results that evening. My test was negative and Christeen's positive. Panicking, I called the clinic. The nurse explained the PCR test will detect dead Covid cells dating from the ice age. She suggested we administer a home test, and if that was negative, return to the clinic in the morning for their version of the home test. We did that and Christeen got a negative result just in time to make our flight from St George.

When HAL reserved our airline flights last August, we were on "red eye," arriving FLL at 7:00 am. Then a few weeks ago, American changed our flights to arrive at 1:00 am. Holland America expressed regret that all airport area hotels were already fully booked. We'd have to spend the night in the airport. (We could've demanded a flight change, but given the air traffic mess over the holidays, it would've been hopeless.)

Our delayed flight arrived at 1:30 am, and we searched for a quiet, dark corner. Unfortunately, all dark corners featured loud PA speakers and lights activated by motion detectors. The last flight out of FLL departed at 2:00 am and annoying Christmas music streamed overhead, interrupted by instructions to "secure our belongings and report any questionable behavior." Then another interruption to "beware of human trafficking in Broward County." Then another interruption by Mayor Lamar Fisher to welcome us to Broward County and assure us there was "something for everyone" here. Repeated through the night. At around 3:30 early bird passengers began arriving for morning flights, and we gave up on sleep.

Shortly before 11:00 we were bused from FLL to the ship terminal and we sleep-walked through a long and winding embarkation line. Without examining our test results, the Covid clerk waved us on to check in. After two hours in the waiting room, attitude-adjusted by warm Holland America cookies, we finally boarded the Zuiderdam, staggered directly to stateroom 8034, and slept.

We awoke just before dinner and surveyed our 174-square-foot stateroom with a balcony. Our accommodations include a queen-size bed, compact loveseat with an oval table, a tiny desk and chair, flat screen TV, and two small wardrobe closets. The bathroom features a single sink, medicine cabinet, head and tub/shower combo with a plastic curtain. I put my arm around Christeen and welcomed her to our new home. She seemed somewhat bewildered. I suggested we go to dinner.

Outside the door we happily found the four suitcases we hadn't seen since December 14th. We secured our face masks and walked the length of the ship, then down the stairs to the formal dining room on deck 2, aft. We were seated at a large table with 4 other couples. Following introductions, we spent the rest of the evening listening to 6 survivors of the "2020 world" describe how the outbreak of Covid had terminated that cruise. And how, after several days anchored outside Perth, Australia, they were finally allowed to disembark. Those who had arranged travel through HAL were promptly assisted with return flights. Those traveling on their own shared various returning-home horror stories. Happily, all of them eventually made it home and were now delighted to be comped on this, the first Holland America world cruise since Covid.

After dinner I hoisted our luggage on the bed and we stuffed our warm weather clothing in the tiny closets. All cool weather clothing, jackets and sweaters we left in the suitcases, and pushed them under the bed. Still exhausted, we tumbled into a gently rocking slumber.

We're off to see the world.

Saint Peter's Anglican Church

Outside and Inside Falmouth, Jamaica

Friday, January 6th

This morning I awoke finally free of travel-induced sleep deprivation. From our veranda, seagulls glided along the bow, surfing the up draft, scanning the Lido deck for errant french fries. Suddenly, a lead gull spied sushi swimming underwater, broke hard right and dove into the swirling ocean. Instantly, the wingman and two others followed. Bam! Bam! Bam! The surface swallowed each with barely a ripple. I gave them a "10." Clearly Chinese gulls.

Yesterday, the manicured new Port at Falmouth featured cobblestone walkways, tourism kiosks, local crafts vendors, diamond and jewelry shops, a pulsating Reggae band, spotless public restrooms and a strangely shuttered Margaritaville Cafe. The port was enclosed within a wrought iron-gated concrete-block fence. Sharply uniformed security staff politely answered questions and gave directions into Falmouth. They also curtly turned away curious locals, oddly unwelcome inside.

Beyond the gate, a different world. Narrow, pot-holed streets were choked with fuming cars, carts, bikes, motorbikes and Jamaicans. Reggae blared from grimy, moldy storefronts. Since there were no street signs anywhere, we asked directions to St Peter's Anglican Church, circa 1750. Twice we were sent the wrong way. Maybe we didn't understand. We finally found the weathered church, survivor of centuries of tropical storms. Inside, Jesus and his disciples, in stained glass, towered above the historic chapel filled with worship-worn pews. We conversed with the eager volunteer sisters at the door, then left a modest contribution.

On the walk back to port, a bare headed young man on a motorbike with no muffler, twisted the throttle and wheelied toward me on the narrow street. No protective clothing, just flip flops, shorts and an old t-shirt. I gave him a thumbs up and a silent prayer as he roared past, front wheel spinning aloft. At the end of the block, he dropped the front wheel and careened around a city bus, its horn blaring and brakes screeching. He pirouetted to the left and disappeared behind the bus. The power of prayer. Or not.

The majority of Jamaicans are descendants of Africans brought to the island by slave trade beginning in the 16th century. Their slave progenitors were purchased by wealthy British sugar cane plantation owners. Later, slaves not sold in Jamaica were sent to plantations in the American south. Jamaicans are beautiful people, proud of their island heritage. It'd been quite warm walking around Falmouth, and by the time we arrived back at the port, it was around 80 degrees. I asked the young Jamaican gate attendant how hot it gets in August. She looked me over, smiled and said, "Very hot. So hot that if you spent the month of August here, you'd look just like me."

Postscript: During our Falmouth walkabout, we chanced upon a small park opposite a dilapidated mansion. Being somewhat footsore, I found a bench under the sole shade tree. Then I noted gazillions of half inch ant-like creatures underfoot. I quickly aborted the rest stop. Back on ship, I found my ankles covered with red blotches. By morning, both calves were covered. The following day, both legs from knees to ankles were covered in swollen blotches. I had wisely packed insect repellent and unwisely left it on the shelf.

"Rainforest Walk, Canal Cruise and Countryside"

Saturday, January 7th

"Rainforest Walk, Canal Cruise and Countryside" described our Holland America excursion, but there was no "countryside" aspect. The rainforest and canal cruise were both within the city limits of Puerto Limon, Costa Rica. And the rainforest required no machete bushwacking. Instead, we shuffled along a broad, rutted dirt path in a local park, beneath a dappled forest canopy. Despite the urban setting, we saw a female howler monkey and her baby in the greenery above, together with some dangling sloths here and there. We also encountered a female golden orb spider, which our guide described as "frequently cannibalizing males both before and during copulation." The ladies in our group were particularly taken by this charming serial killer.

Following the rainforest, we boarded a weary flat-bottomed dinghy, which appeared safe for maybe half of us. To avoid swamping, we were instructed to sit on alternating sides of the craft. Once loaded, the hull of the dinghy sank to a scant 18 inches above the murky mosquito-mating water line. Thankfully, most mosquitoes had the day off. During our cruise we saw more sloths and howler monkeys, together with some rare blue herons and a couple of sunbathing iguanas. Sadly, we missed the Cayman alligator seen by the morning group.

As we disembarked, I noticed life jackets safely stowed under the seats and wondered why we weren't instructed to wear them in this gator-infested swamp. Then it occurred to me: if anyone had toppled overboard, the captain would likely have lost a perfectly good life jacket.

Guide in Puerto Limon rainforest

Panama Canal from Sea to Shining Sea

Sunday, January 8th

I read David McCullough's seminal history of the Panama Canal, *The Path Between the Seas,* before our first canal cruise in 2008, and Holland America kindly provided a refresher lecture. In 1881, France began constructing a canal in the Chagres River, but subsequently abandoned the project after an unimaginable loss of lives and fortunes. America took over in 1904, and through engineering genius, the conquest of mosquito-borne diseases and the tenacity of Teddy Roosevelt, the canal was completed in 1914. The 108 year-old locks system was an engineering marvel then and remains so today. In the years since, the impact of a waterway between the oceans has transformed the world economy.

The wide Chagres River hosted a flotilla of cargo vessels on this pleasant Sunday morning. Dozens of container ships awaited a spot in the locks. There are a total of 12 locks in the canal system, which elevate each vessel 54 feet above sea level. In adjacent locks, the Zuiderdam and its sister ship the Volendam (enroute to Antarctica) slowly rose to the level of the next lock. This is Holland America's 150th Anniversary year, and Captain Friso said the Zuiderdam and the Volendam, together in the locks, gave him goosebumps.

As we sailed out of the locks, I spied a golden angel Moroni trumpeting across leafy hilltops on the port side. The Latter-day Saints are marching into Panama. Beyond Moroni across the treetops, endless skyscrapers glistened in the afternoon sun. The Panama City skyline reminded me of Shanghai, with tower cranes and skyscrapers cluttering the horizon. Panama City has undergone a stunning transformation in the years since Jimmy Carter signed a new canal treaty in 1977, which granted full canal sovereignty to Panama in 1999.

Over the intercom, cruise director Ian has just drawn our attention to two adult crocodiles sunbathing on the sandy riverbank, starboard side. I think I'll take my dips in the pool.

The Volendam in the locks

Fuerte Amador, Panamá

Monday, January 9

Fuerte Amador (strong lover in Spanish) is the port at the Pacific entrance to the Panama canal. It's made up of a one-mile causeway connecting four small islands and extending out into the Pacific. We had the option of taking a shuttle to one of the islands called Perico (parakeet in Spanish), or another bus to The Multiplaza shopping mall in Panama City. I almost had my shop-till-you-drop esposa convinced to go parakeeting until we happened upon cruise director Ian. "The Multiplaza mall is a must see," he said. Accordingly, we took the scenic 40-minute bus ride into Panama City.

We were told the Zuiderdam paid over $400,000 in tolls to transit the canal yesterday. A breathtaking sum. But compared to the cost of sailing 1400 guests and 800 crew around Cape Horn for another three weeks? You do the math. Money is flowing into Panama, and in The Multiplaza, wealthy Panamanians are spending it. Soaring ceilings, gleaming marble floors, glittering storefronts, an expansive food court, three levels of shopping and an ice-skating rink. It oozes Beverly Hills class, with no vacant storefronts. Returning canal sovereignty to Panama has had a profound impact on job creation and economic development here. The poverty rate has decreased from 48% in 1991 to just 12% in 2019. Panama is on the move.

I let Christeen forage The Marketplace on her own and did a lap of the mall perimeter out in the tropical sun. Back on ship an hour later, the skies quickly darkened, and suddenly a fiery blast rocked the Zuiderdam. I thought a bomb had exploded. On the intercom Captain

Friso confirmed a direct lightning strike, destroying an antenna. Hopefully not the GPS antenna. With 8 sea days to Polynesia, we'd rather not end up in Manila.

Panama City skyline

Taiohae, Nuku Hiva

Wednesday, January 18th

We have frustratingly crossed the serene Pacific without internet service or texting. To mollify annoyed cruisers, Holland America has refunded 6 days internet fees for the Pacific "dead zone." Are there no satellites above the Pacific?

Just before sunrise, Captain Friso handed the wheel over to a local pilot who deftly slipped the Zuiderdam into Taiohae Bay, Nuku Hiva, the largest of the Marquesas Islands in French Polynesia. The bay is lined with natural rocky outcroppings slathered in desert scrub vegetation. From atop the Lido deck, ornery rain clouds wrap the top of the island. I scanned the vertical rock-faced shoreline with binoculars. Not a beach in sight. The lady standing next to me murmured, "It looks like a giant reptile asleep on the water."

Nuku Hiva is an arid island bisected by a gnarly jeep trail across a 4,000-foot mountain top. The total island population per the 2017 census is around 3,000, with most in Taiohae. It's a south pacific rainforest without rain or forest: hot, humid and yet summerly parched. Cruise ships in Taiohae Bay are recent and rare. Tourist infrastructure is wanting. There are no white sand beaches, no glass-bottom boats, no tour buses, no Hilton Resort Hotels or any hotels. Only a smattering of rental bungalows and guest cottages.

Disembarking ship passengers nearly doubled the population of Taiohae. We took a tender to the dock and were greeted by morning quiet, politely interrupted by distant percussive Polynesian rumba. We walked past a makeshift craft market, shading a handful of local artisans and fruit vendors. Compact 4x4 pickups and an occasional minivan or scooter quietly motored back and forth along the bayfront road. Chickens and goats wandered aimlessly. A dozen or so catamarans, sails stowed, picturesquely listed in the painterly bay. The kind of place to disappear in.

In June 1842 Herman Melville wrote that the beauty of the Taiohae harbor "was lost to me then," since he was focused on six passing French warships. After the warships sailed on, Melville stayed long enough to write portions of his novel *Typee*, and immerse himself in the beauty of Taiohae Bay. Today, the bay remains secretly sublime in the absence of obsessive tourism. The island hasn't fully tapped the economic potential of cruise ships. Once it does, Nuku Hiva may become paradise lost.

Taiohae Bay, Nuku Hiva

Sublime Sea Days

Friday, January 20th

We've been on the blue Pacific for 10 of the past 11 days. Lazy clouds and blissful breezes have been our seafaring companions. With nary a passing ship, we've had the peaceful Pacific to ourselves.

Before embarking, Christeen worried she'd be pushed to the brink on boring sea days. That hasn't been a problem. The daily activity calendar is loaded, and days have passed quickly. To help keep us grounded, HAL places "day of the week" mats in each elevator. We are sailing west, which means about every other evening, Captain Friso orders clocks set back an hour. More divine sleep in this floating cradle.

There have been daily lectures on ship building, naval warfare, the universe, quantum theory, oceanic flora and fauna, whaling, surfing and world travel. Beyond the lectures, there are classes for poker, bridge, drawing, watercolor, art history, pickleball, ballroom dance, creative writing, Tai Chi, knitting, needlework, ukulele, line dancing, Polynesian dance, aerobics, origami folding, yoga, stretching, shabbat, Catholic mass and devotions. Plus, daily games of bridge, poker, chess, dominos, Mahjong, trivial pursuit, bingo, charades, shuffleboard, ping pong, basketball and more. A new library stocked with reference books and best sellers just opened on deck three. Dozens of movies and several news networks are available on stateroom televisions. Nightly Mainstage productions feature music, dance and comedy. There are music venues for rock n' roll, contemporary jazz, classic strings and piano. In addition, the Zuiderdam features a full casino, several shops, an art gallery, a gym, a spa and two swimming pools with four hot tubs. If none of that interests you, check your pulse. You're probably dead.

The food on board has been fresh, varied, plentiful and consistently good. We expected to see some cruise ship gluttony, but second helpings are rare, single scoop portions are preferred and default desserts are "no sugar added." Most world cruisers are long haulers, too experienced to over-indulge. Still, preventing cruise ship body-wrecking requires some self control and elevator avoidance.

Of the 1,400 guests on the ship, it seems more than half are repeat world cruises, some a dozen times or more. The typical age ranges from the 60s through early 90s. Several employ canes, walkers, wheelchairs or scooters. There are comparatively few poolside loungers. Swimmers often wear hats and sunbathers are rare and modestly covered. Sounds boring, but it's quite the opposite. We're surrounded by fascinating, friendly people with interesting life experiences. One couple brought four pre-teen adopted daughters that they're homeschooling on board. Those charming little girls must have won the parent-picking sweepstakes.

For some, world cruising offers advantages over retirement homes. One retirement home resident said she saves $1,000 a month while aboard ship. And no retirement home can match cruise ship food, service, entertainment and scenery. The waiters, stewards, and other service staff are typically from Indonesia or the Philippines. They work hard, never complain and are always happy, helpful and considerate. They remember our names and brighten our days. Plus, there's a hospital, resident doctor and nursing staff on board. All for less per month than many retirement homes.

It's a no brainer.

Papeete and Moorea Revisited

Sunday, January 22nd

The correct pronunciation of Moorea requires the O hop: MO'O-ray-ah. Papeete is Papa-A-tay. From atop the Lido deck Moorea is stunning this morning. Lush tropical foliage carpets the island from seashore to mountaintop. No rocky outcroppings and nothing barren.

Upon first sight of this botanical wonderland in September 1777, Captain Cook and his starving sailors must have experienced a collective foodie orgasm. Plentiful bananas, breadfruit, yams, taro and coconuts to turn the tide of ravaging scurvy. After months at sea, gagging on moldy biscuits and rancid bacon, they'd found paradise. With naked women. In my binoculars, the lush Moorea shoreline scene is interspersed with white coral beaches and thatched bungalows. But no naked women. Captain Frisco has anchored the Zuiderdam at the entrance to a winding cove. It's shortly after 7:00 am, and the ship's tenders are launched. Unfortunately, Christeen remains luxuriantly asleep.

Yesterday downtown Papeete had an unsettling third-world vibe: noisy traffic, seedy storefronts and sidewalks lined with homeless men and women. "Homeless Tahitian?" Sounds like an oxymoron. Don't most Polynesians live in grass huts and subsist on breadfruit and bananas? How could anyone be homeless here?

The walkway from the cruise ship terminal led toward a massive two-story, open-air "Marketplace." Local artisans, farmers, fishermen, fast foodies, jewelers, toymakers, bakers and dressmakers plied wares in the crowded Marketplace. Outside, homeless people on the sidewalks seemed out of character for Polynesia and the Papeete we visited 40 years ago. A few blocks away, we happened upon a modest circa 1875 Catholic cathedral, refreshingly cool and quiet inside. Later, in the leafy afternoon, we found a shady harborside pedestrian park. The park would've been far lovelier than the busy Marketplace to direct disembarking visitors. But parks don't contribute much to the local economy.

In many ways, Moorea is an island apart from Papeete: serene and laid-back with unspoiled natural beauty. We were told half the workers on Moorea take a 30 to 40-minute ferry to Papeete for work, which leaves the island unexpectedly quiet. We hired a driver and did an island lap, stopping at *South Pacific* and *Mutiny on the Bounty* film sites. It rained intermittently in Moorea all day, from light sprinkles to a brief monsoon. Sweet soaking rain, feeding lush foliage and tropical rust.

On the tender back to the ship, we sat across from Tom and Mary from Stillwater, Oklahoma. I mentioned Oklahoma is home to country music stars like Garth Brooks, Vince Gill and Merle Haggard. Tom grinned and added Reba McIntyre, Toby Keith, Blake Shelton and others. Tom attended the same high school as Vince Gill, and Tom's sister was pals with Gill's sister. One day, the girls and young Vince with his guitar visited Tom when he was at OSU. Vince told Tom he was going to be a country music star. "Regrettably," Tom said, "I didn't pay much attention to him. He was just a junior high kid."

On the Mainstage tonight we were treated to the "Tahitian Folklore Show." It featured a dozen native drummers pounding on gourds, with a troupe of scantily clad Polynesian dancers titillating. Delicate hands caressed invisible waves, while swaying bosoms and gyrating hips incinerated the stage. They turned their finest ass-ets to the audience and stepped on the gas. It was sensory overload; my circuits shorted and I fell asleep. A few minutes later I awoke to boisterous clapping by the guy next to me. As the drummers sent the dancers' bosoms and bottoms back into orbit, I drifted back to sweet slumber. Until the clapper lunged for the standing ovation.

Moorea

Oyster farm, Raiatea

Raiatea, Society Islands

Monday, January 23rd

Our itinerary had us in Bora Bora today. However, Bora Bora is apparently refusing large cruise ships. Why? Bora Bora is tiny, comprising only 38-square kilometers. It's likely the negative impacts of hundreds of cruisers disembarking on the tiny island. That's understandable. However, no worries. Raiatea is another island gem, and we're happy to spend an extra day here.

We enjoyed lunch today with Rita, a delightfully lithe, white haired 90-year-old diva, who is doing her 8th world cruise. She is a Floridian with ocean blue eyes, a contented smile and deeply carved bronze skin. After a lite lunch, she gazed longingly out the rain-splattered window and mused, "I've snorkeled all along those reefs, and when the weather clears, I'm anxious to get back out there." I told her I'd heard someone on the ship has completed 22 world cruises. She said she knew someone who has done 40. Last year, she did 5 shorter cruises before embarking on this one.
"They'll never put me in a retirement home," she declared.

Tuesday, January 24th

During our drive along the east coast of Raiatea this morning, our narrator struggled with English and a scratchy microphone. We didn't understand much, but it didn't matter. If Moorea is the prettiest island, Raiatea may be first runner-up. We visited a lush, fragrant botanical garden teeming with strange colorful species. We stopped at a sacred archeology site and were served platters of fresh pineapple, mango, grapefruit and watermelon, together with a refreshing open-top coconut on ice. The LDS prophet Joseph Smith taught that the Garden of Eden was near Jackson County, Missouri. I've been there, and I've been here. And I've never seen a Missouri garden look anything like this. Must be climate change.

Many Raiatea dwellings are little more than shanties with corrugated fiberglass or galvanized metal roofs. No insulation, no heating and no cooling. Windows and doors stand wide open. Laundry pinned to clotheslines flutters in the breeze. People sit on steps with front doors open; domestic animals and chickens run freely in and around houses surrounded by wild natural greenery. Oddly, there seems to be as many shanties along the ocean as on the opposite side of the road. There are some fine homes, of course, but even those are rather modest. There's something special about life on Raiatea. Nature provides the basics for living. Beyond that, what matters?

Back at the bay, I met a young American investment banker who bought a tawdry sailing yacht in Raiatea a few years ago. Now he spends 9 months of the year anchored in the bay, restoring the vessel for a future Pacific crossing. He chose Raiatea for its unspoiled beauty and laid back lifestyle. If all of Polynesia were geographically more accessible to Europe and the Americas, it would be overrun with mega-yachts, casinos, movie stars, jet setters, A-listers and Formula One.

Thankfully, the Almighty isolated Polynesia in its own world.

Papeete

The Band

Rolling Stone Lounge and the Fabulous Finkel

Wednesday, January 25th

We are back at sea with a scheduled arrival in Tonga early next Monday. We'll cross the International Date Line on Friday and skip Saturday. After a Mainstage production a couple weeks ago, we checked out the band in Rolling Stone Lounge. They played 60s, 70s and 80s rock n' roll in 45-minute sets, with 15-minute breaks. I was stunned by the soaring lead vocals, perfect harmonies, crisp percussion and spot-on guitar, keyboard and bass solos. After the first set, I asked Leo, the lead guitar player, the name of the band. He said, "We don't have a name; just call us "The Band." One night last week Leo broke a string at the end of his solo on Springsteen's "Born to Run." The lead singer laughed nervously and asked, "How long will it take to fix that?" Leo replied, "120 seconds." Turns out he was slow, someone in the crowd timed him. It took just 150 seconds to replace the string, tune the guitar and dive into the intro to Santana's "Black Magic Woman."

Elliot Finkel, a pianist from Brooklyn, New York, headlined the Mainstage last week. When he walked on the stage blowing kisses to the ladies, he didn't look like a concert pianist. He's a big man with snowy locks and lumberjack hands. He looked like he could've played on the o-line, protecting Joe Namath's wobbly knees, during the glory days of the New York Jets. But make no mistake, Finkel is a fabulous pianist. Maybe too fabulous. He faced a glistening ebony Steinway Grand and gently fondled the keys for a few melodic bars. Ladies in the audience swooned at a familiar Broadway show tune. Then all hell broke loose. Finkel's flying fingers flitted across the keys, danced hand over hand, slid across the octaves, tip-toed the high notes, hammered the low notes, then slithered back and forth across the keyboard again and again. Finally, having obliterated the song, Finkel stood, faced the audience and flung his head back and hands in the air, beaming. The dazed audience politely applauded. Finkel had just beat the crap out of the Steinway. In fact, some tech guy in overalls came on stage after Finkel's third song, stuck his head under the lid and performed some emergency repairs. Befuddled, Finkel muttered, "Hey, whatcha doin' under there?" After the repairs, Finkel completed his show in the same indulgent fashion. Listening to Finkel reminded me of 20 minute guitar solos by Jimmy Hendrix. I appreciated talent, but enough is enough.

Later in the week, Finkel played a lovely classical set in the Explorer Lounge. This time, he stuck to the script and played the songs as they were written. On the Mainstage he proved he was a great pianist. In the Explorer Lounge he proved he could make beautiful music.

We returned to the Rolling Stone Lounge tonight after a talented saxophonist did an impressive, if forgettable, show on the Mainstage. In the Lounge, we were surprised that The Band's female singer had disembarked in Papeete. She's been replaced by a second lead guitarist who sings tenor. This was the new guy's first set with bandmates he met 4 days ago. Tonight they did superb covers of Cream, The Kinks, Aerosmith, Fleetwood Mac, Toto, Looking Glass, Kansas and others. They finished with Led Zeppelin's, "Stairway to Heaven." I thought they were going to blow the roof off deck two. Were Jimmy Page and John Bonham on board, I think they'd have joined in the standing ovation. It gave me goosebumps.

Lapping the Zuiderdam

Sunday, January 29th

My body tells me it's Saturday; however, we just crossed the International Date Line and Captain Friso says it's Sunday.

On sea day mornings, I walk (clop, actually) 6 laps around the Promenade Deck, equivalent to 2 miles. I walk early, before the fitness freaks crowd the deck, use my walking stick for balance and give passers a wide berth. Smooth seas have accommodated my clopping. So far, I haven't decked anyone or myself. My pace is glacial: generally 6:45 to 7:15 per lap, or about 21 minutes a mile. I rarely pass anyone; even the plus size bodies lap me at will. But I love getting out, inhaling fresh ocean air and watching the sun rise above deep indigo on a clear morning. My fellow walkers are eccentric. They include a speed walker, flapping his arms and dog paddling the wind, a tiny oriental lady scooting around like a bow-legged ladybug and an aging statuesque distance runner effortlessly passing lap after lap.

The other day, a yoga-spandexed, sixty-something blonde slowed as she approached from behind, "Did you break your right leg some time ago?"

"No, it's muscle atrophy."

"What causes that?" she asked, slowing to my clop.

"Neuropathy."

She looked me up and down, her blonde curls brushing her eyebrows in the breeze. Suddenly, her eyes widened, "If you weren't walking, you'd be in a wheelchair!" she exclaimed, striding away.

Clever girl.

Today we're sailing toward an ominous cloud homesteading the horizon. The seas are swelling moderately. I was out at 5:30 this morning and joined only a handful of other walkers. My pace was slower than usual, clopping up and down and balancing side to side as the Zuiderdam pitched and rolled. Between my unsteady clop and my flailing stick, I expected some wiseacre to shout from behind, "On your right, Ahab!" I have a ready response: "That's Captain Ahab to you, Pequod!" (Yes, Pequod was the name of the ship, but it has a suitably snarky ring to it.)

Muted Tonga

Tuesday, January 31st

Yesterday morning, after threatening rain, the skies over Tongatapu island cleared quickly. The temperature rose to 85 degrees, with humidity at a super sweaty 100 percent. Together with three other couples, we combed the dock at Nuku'alofa for an island tour. Virginia, a Chinese woman in our group, badgered a tour operator until she obtained a $20 per person discount. It was slightly embarrassing, but we happily paid the reduced fare. Then we discovered we had rented a rusty old van and a speechless driver. Virginia rode shotgun, and the rest of us piled in back, with me and Christeen in the rear. Almost instantly, we were sweating profusely. Once underway, the geriatric air conditioner dropped the inside van temperature from sweltering to slow roast.

Our stocky, fifty-something driver, dressed in a Tonga-traditional white shirt, black skirt and thatched apron, spoke not a word as we set off through town.

We questioned aloud: "Does anyone know where we're going?"

"What's that building on the left?"

"Is that an Anglican church?"

Our driver remained morbidly mute. Finally, Virginia confronted him in her shrill Mandarin-English: "Don't you know you're supposed to narrate?" He glanced aside, mumbled some unintelligible Tonglish and drove on. After several similarly enlightening exchanges, Virginia resorted to sign language. She placed her Tonga map in his face, pointed to an attraction and asked, "Next stop?" Eyes on the road, hands on the wheel, he occasionally grunted "yes," or "no" as our mobile sauna baked down the road.

Unlike mountainous French Polynesia, Tongatapu is flat, but still lush and humid. I was here 25 years ago, investigating a potential investment in aloe vera. The island is busier than I remember, but the essential character seems unchanged. Last November, a 7.3-magnitude earthquake occurred 130 miles off the coast of Tongatapu, creating a tsunami on the island. But today little residual damage is evident. The homes are island modest, similar to Polynesia, with laundry humidifying on clotheslines and dogs, chickens and pigs lazing about rusty old cars and cluttering junk. This amidst unimaginably glorious tropical vegetation, pristine coral beaches, and sweetly calming island breezes. Paradise, populated.

We were silently delivered to all major Tongatapu tourist attractions: the flying fruit bats, the blowholes, Captain Cook's landing place, the terraced tombs and the ancient tsunami stone. I was unprepared for our final stop, the Anahulu Stalactite Cave. The fee, for which Virginia deftly negotiated a 33% discount, was posted outside a leaning entry shack. The cave was a certifiable OSHA-ADA nightmare. Steep, narrowly irregular stone steps, covered in wet sand descended sharply toward a dark cavern. No safety instructions, no handrails, no paint stripes and no lights on the descent. The deep cavern below was dimly lit by random flickering lamps. We gingerly slid down the slippery steps into a wide, ghoulish cavern, ceilings about 40 feet high with dripping stalactites. As my dilated eyes adjusted to the pallid lighting on the rock walls, I heard a loud BOOM, then another, followed by lively chatter. Teenage Tongans were diving and cannonballing from a rock ledge 25 feet above a black pond at the bottom of the cavern. It seemed crazy dangerous and I thought, *"Isn't this a school day?"*

If Tonga were part of the USA, I'm sure trial lawyers would have kiosks adjacent to the entry shack at Anahulu Cave promising, "We don't get paid until you get paid!" But since Anahulu Cave is privately operated and likely not insured, there wouldn't be anyone to pay those angelic attorneys for the unfortunate slips and falls. Enter at your own risk.

Due to a passing squall, we were delayed 30 minutes in Nuku'alofa last night before sailing for Auckland, New Zealand. This morning the seas were the heaviest yet, the ship pitching and rolling like a gastric rhino. I woke at 4:45, debated giving my peg leg the day off, read the digital Wall Street Journal, dozed a bit and then descended 5 floors to deck 3 at about 6:30. Deck traffic was light, as many cruisers, dehydrated yesterday by tropical Tonga, were probably still asleep. I did a lot of sidestep-balance clopping on the swaying deck but completed my 2 miles without incident.

Tonga blowholes

Albert Park

Auckland and Tauranga

Auckland is a harbor city on the north island of New Zealand with a metro area population of nearly 1.7 million. The architecture is an eclectic mix of historic and modern dating from the late 18th and early 19th centuries. Upon disembarking yesterday morning, we walked a few blocks to the Explorer Bus double decker. Auckland is cosmopolitan, leafy green and strikingly clean, with handsome men and women strolling the sidewalks amid gleaming office towers and alluring shops, clubs and cafes. We made our first stop at the Auckland Art Gallery and Albert Park. The gallery dates to the 1890s and today occupies an architecturally magnificent four-story structure which opened in 2011. The adjacent Albert Park rises on a hill above the museum and is a botanical beauty with a bandstand, an 1880s fountain, historic bronze statues, radiant flower gardens, blooming magnolias and towering sycamores.

Inside the gallery, an excellent exhibition of elderly Māori native portraits by New Zealand artist Charles F. Goldie. Unfortunately, exhibitions of works by Frida Kahlo, Diego Rivera and New Zealand painter Dame Robin White, closed last week. Hence, two main exhibit halls were closed for changeout. In the remaining galleries, the museum appeared to follow the current trend toward "edgy" contemporary art — much of which, in my view, is contemporary crap. After walking each floor, we retreated to the Gallery Café for a soda and éclair. I'm an éclair junkie and that chocolate-free éclair was a world beater: light and creamy, with intensely delicious berry dabs.

We made other stops at the Auckland Museum, the Holy Trinity Cathedral (closed, unfortunately), the quaint Parnell Shopping District, and the Downtown Market Plaza. All made for a nice walkabout, but only a taste of a great city. Auckland is a place to come back to.

Tauranga

Tauranga, New Zealand, is situated on a narrow spit of land, sandwiched by the blue south Pacific ocean. It's home to around 137,000 (2018 census), but you'd never guess that from the bay view. A deep harbor anchors the west side. To the east, a white coral beach fronts a gaggle of surfers bobbing in the swells. Mount Maunganui crowns the northern tip. The place is achingly beautiful, with glass-front homes and low-rise condos basking in idyllic bay views, gentle sea breezes and lapping tides. It seems too perfect, actually.

We walked the 3.4-kilometer trail around the jagged coastline of Mount Maunganui. The mountain is surrounded by ocean; only about 30 of its 360-degree perimeter touches land. The remainder is licked by the warm South Pacific. On the trail, we happened upon a couple of talkative kiwis. The woman said it had been raining steadily for the past week. Indeed, the trail was soggy underfoot, but well drained. She said she was a chef. When asked the best place for great New Zealand lamb, she replied, "That would be in the UK, mate. We ship all our best lamb to the Brits."

I took dozens of photos along the trail. The view beyond every bend begged for brush and canvas. Exiting the trail, we followed the beach to the shops along Maunganui Road. We bought a cold soda and ordered fish and chips and fried oysters at a nondescript seafood takeaway. The food was served in baskets on newspaper, perfectly fried and delicious. Christeen spent the balance of the afternoon shopping for New Zealand wear, while I browsed a local bookshop and then walked.

So little time; so much pretty.

Back on ship, we dined on surf n turf, filet mignon and grilled garlic shrimp, followed by warm rhubarb crisp and vanilla ice cream. On the Mainstage, Debora Krizak, a slithering blue-sequined Australian, sweetly sang Helen Reddy, Tina Turner, Olivia Newton John, Dolly Parton, Adele and others. On our stateroom TV we watched the movie *Crocodile Dundee*, and then drifted off to the land down under. Less than a week away....

It's a wonderful life.

Mount Maunganui trail

Rodney and Lynette

Saturday, February 4th

After a perfect day in the coastal logging town of Gisborne (Gizzy to the locals), we shared dinner on the Lido deck with a pair of kiwis, Rodney and Lynette, who are retired dairy farmers from a rural area two hours south of here. They didn't bother getting off ship today, as they'd "Been to Gizzy a hundred times." They embarked on the Zuiderdam in Ft Lauderdale, like most of us. I asked Rodney if he knew of Bert Munro, the motorcycle racer played by Anthony Hopkins in *The World's Fastest Indian*. He knew all about Munro, and then said two of his sons were retired motorcycle racers, one in Moto GP and the other in hill climb. I recall as a teenager some of the world's best motocross racers were New Zealanders. Rodney's boys were apparently both expert racers, and both got banged up along the way.
"Thankfully, they both survived racing," he said.

I asked them about Chris Hipkins, the newly sworn New Zealand Prime Minister (after the recent resignation of Jacinda Ardern).

"Couldn't be much worse than the last one. Just trading one liar for another, mate," Rodney replied.

"But the news media in America characterized Ardern as beloved in her country and respected the world over." I said.

"Rubbish!" he declared. "Before she took over, our country was near debt-free. Now because of her crushing Covid lockdowns we're buried in debt, the economy's ruined and many businesses are bankrupt." Lynette frowned and nodded approvingly.

"But our media fawned over Prime Minister Arden as a hero, one who led the world in Covid response and saved her country during the pandemic. Then resigned, as she said, "for the good of the country, as there was no gas left in her tank.""

Rodney grunted. "She never had any gas in her tank, mate. Before becoming Prime Minister, her business experience was as an order-taker for a fish and chips takeaway. She quit because she was getting lots of hate mail."

"What about the media portrayal of her as superwoman, since she had a baby while Prime Minister?" I asked.

"Yeah, she had a baby all right, with her boyfriend. She turned the little bugger over to a nanny. Then her boyfriend straightaway knockered up the nanny. People here are fed up with her lying and covering the truth and the mess she's left us in."

It also annoyed Rodney and Lynette that, during the pandemic, deaths of old people with pre-existing conditions were invariably reported in New Zealand as Covid deaths. Their daughter-in-law, a hospital nurse in Wellington, surmised it was because "Covid" is easier to spell than "pneumonia."

Our new kiwi friends confirmed a couple of things: 1) politics and politicians are unloved everywhere, and 2) dairy farmers don't have much use for either. Unless of course, the topic is dairy subsidies, or proposed government regulations.

We're off to windy Wellington.

Te Papa Museum "Gallipoli" exhibit

Windy Wellington

Sunday, February 5th

New Zealanders correctly call their capital city "windy Wellington." It's been wet and blustery all day here. Captain Friso just announced we are sailing into a cold front with expected 12-foot swells and gale force winds. We've been ordered off the decks and advised to hang on to the rails. Seems like a welcome change, after South Pacific heat and humidity.

This morning we rode a historic cable car up a steep grade to the Wellington Botanical Garden at the top of Kelburn Lookout. We've toured several lovely New Zealand botanical gardens, and they're almost redundant as New Zealand *is* a botanical garden. The panoramic views from Kelburn Lookout over the city center and across Wellington Harbor were magical. We toured the historic Cable Car Museum and then took a winding path through the 25-hectare Wellington Garden, replete with exotic plants, strange native trees, colorfully themed floral plots and the 300-variety Lady Norwood Rose Garden.

At the end of the rose garden, we entered the Bolton Street Cemetery, a dappled resting place for generations of deceased Wellingtoners. Tilting, moss-covered headstones marked the historic gravesites. Outside the cemetery, we crossed a pedestrian bridge over a motorway, and the cemetery reappeared on the opposite side. What?

In 1968, hundreds of graves were exhumed and re-interred in a large vault behind the Cemetery Museum to make way for a new freeway. Imagine getting a freeway approved through Forest Lawn in Los Angeles? Never happen. Probably never happen again in New Zealand, either. We ate lunch at a windy harborside brew pub, then crossed the dock to the

Te Papa Museum of New Zealand. Te Papa is a gem, with 5 floors of art and cultural displays, plus an observation deck. The museum highlight is "Gallipoli," an exhibit honoring New Zealand soldiers who joined Allied forces in an amphibious landing at Gallipoli peninsula during World War I. The campaign was orchestrated by the then First Lord of the Admiralty, Winston Churchill, with the objective of weakening the Ottoman Empire and protecting the Allied supply route through the Suez Canal. After eight months fighting, the campaign failed and was considered a huge defeat for Churchill and the Allies. Ultimately it provided the basis for the Turkish War of Independence eight years later. Of the 15,000 New Zealand soldiers who participated, over half were killed or wounded.

The Gallipoli exhibit is indescribably powerful and poignant. It proceeds through a dozen or so rooms, tracing the entire nine months of the conflict. The exhibit displays several soldiers and a nurse, all cast in resin 2.4 times human size. The figures and their uniforms, boots, buttons, belts, weapons, hats, c-rations, canteens, machine guns, watches and helmets are all rendered giant-sized. Providing breathtaking depictions of anger, hatred, fear, dread, terror, sorrow, pain and death. Life details for each person rendered are also exhibited, including family, education, copies of letters to loved ones, military records and ultimate death. "Gallipoli" is a deeply disturbing work of art.

I'd return to Wellington just to see it again.

The Endangered Seven Deadly Sins

Tuesday, February 7th

Since seeing the shuttered Margaritaville Cafe in Jamaica, Jimmy Buffett's "Bank of Bad Habits" has been running through my mind:

Bank of bad habits
The price of vice foretold.
One by one they'll do you in
They're bound to take their toll.

I wonder, do those bad habits (sins) still have traction among aging world cruisers, in various states of piety, health, wealth, mobility and acuity? Or has relentless aging muted the powers of evil?

1. Pride

Who on this ship were homecoming royalty, all-conference quarterbacks, beauty queens, class presidents, CEOs, distinguished faculty or civic leaders? Aging is hardest on the most beautiful, most talented, most athletic and most successful. The rewards of long life include gray hair or no hair, sags and wrinkles and slips and falls. We don't recognize the geezer in the mirror, and sooner or later we don't recognize anyone else, either.

2. Coveting

In a prior day, greed may have driven some to make a fortune, inherit a fortune, steal a fortune or rule over the less fortunate. But here, there are no elections, no money to make and no banks to rob. There's a full casino on deck two, but it's typically as quiet as a nunnery.

3. Lust

The only poolside "look" is likely a blank stare. There are no incredible hulks and no hotties tanning poolside. Of course, there are quite a number of hulks around, but they are not incredible. Bodies are not on display poolside. Towels are.

4. Anger

Face masks were mandatory during the first three weeks of the cruise. One evening, a guest arrived for a lecture (gasp!) maskless. A vigilante masker tapped the offending violator on the shoulder and told him to mask up. The maskless violator ignored the vigilante and took a seat. Presently the exasperated vigilante reached over and tapped the violator again. Instantly the geriatric violator rose from his chair, cane in hand, and bellowed in the face of the vigilante, "You touch me again, and I'll knock your head off!" Thus rebuked, the vigilante sullenly slumped in his seat and ceased tapping. That's the sole display of anger I've seen on this cruise.

5. Gluttony

Dining Room portions are modestly spare. Fresh sweet rolls and sticky buns are not breakfast best sellers. Even so, skinny folks are a minority here. Most of the cruisers have lived the good life and show it. Notwithstanding, gluttony on board seems as enticing as a poolside Polaroid.

6. Envy

Some may own a two-carat diamond or a Patek Philippe watch, but who cares? Most would not pack such non-wearable frivolity. Take it ashore and invite assault.

7. Sloth

Sloth is the scary one. This world cruise shares an uncomfortable parallel with the Disney movie *WALL-E*, where humans were waited on 24/7 by robots. Our service staffers are not robots, but they do almost everything for us. Sloths hang upside down in trees and move *very slowly,* only when required. We are decidedly not sloths, but we admit we move like them.

That's it. The Seven Deadly Sins disembarked in Jamaica. Next port of call: Nirvana. Oops, Jimmy, I almost forgot: the eighth deadly sin is Pizza Hut! Happily, we left them all in Florida.

Above: Sydney Opera House
Below: Sydney skyline

Sydney Before Sunup

Thursday, February 9th

I awakened at 4:00 this morning and was in the Crow's Nest by five for Cruise Director Ian's commentary on Sydney Harbor. Rain in the pre-dawn dark, coupled with the glare of bright lights inside the Crow's Nest made for poor visibility. Undaunted, cheerfully caffeinated Ian narrated the wet black nothingness as we cruised into the harbor. I ventured on deck in the spitting rain for a better look. We passed the famed Sydney Opera House, then cruised under the Sydney Harbor Bridge aka the "Coat Hanger Bridge." There's an excursion offered by Holland America to climb a zillion steps to the top of the Harbor Bridge. (Think climbing to the top of Golden Gate Bridge.) The cost for this exhausting exhilaration? *$499 per person.* I thought it was a misprint. They should pay me $500 to do it. I spoke to a lady (one of five from the ship) who did it. She said the tour required a head-to-toe jumpsuit cabled to the rail. Cabled apparently to preclude suicidal skydiving. Certainly there are cheaper and less exhausting ways to kill oneself.

The misty morning visibility continued throughout the day. Under overcast skies, we visited the Blue Mountains (a UNESCO World Heritage site), a two hour drive from downtown Sydney. We saw dense fog and no blue mountains. Despite the fog, we enjoyed three cable car rides down, up and across the misty Scenic World Park. Later, we savored delicious Aussie-style fried chicken breast over mashed potatoes and gravy in a stately circa 1908 hotel. Christeen said it reminded her of the Hotel Del Coronado. After lunch, we visited Featherdale Wildlife Park, a casual petting zoo teeming with parrots, wombats, kangaroos and koala bears. I knew eucalyptus trees were native to Australia (there are 800 species of eucalyptus, and they're everywhere), but I had no idea that koalas eat *only* eucalyptus leaves. No beef jerky, no tater tots and no Twinkies. Poor little buggers.

Our cheery narrator was unable to describe the fog-shrouded scenery, so she switched to Australian politics. Last year the Aussies *quietly* elected a new Prime Minister. She said American elections remind her of a circus. We collectively agreed. "Australians are required by law to vote," she said. "Refuse to vote? Get a fine. Refuse to pay the fine? The fine is doubled. Continue refusing, the fines and penalties increase until your driver's license expires. Then you pay all fines and all penalties prior to renewal." Additionally, she pointed out there is no voting fraud in Australia. Voters must present picture identification, eliminating duplicate voting. And here's the best part: Aussie candidates do not advertise on TV.

Why not follow the Aussie example? Require all citizens to vote and prohibit TV or radio advertising. Then go a step further: prohibit yard signs, billboards, leaflets and all advertising. Take the money out of politics and make political fundraising illegal. No buying elections. Limit campaigning to debates, personal appearances and writing editorials. All voters would be left to educate themselves. And everyone would vote just once.

It's a fantasy, I know.

Friday, February 10th

The upper deck of a sightseeing bus proved the perfect place to see Sydney on this sumptuous summer morning. Our tour took two hours and during the loop, we heard many folks say "Sydney's my favorite city."

We stopped at the historic St. Mary's Cathedral. Indescribably opulent, its 13th-century Gothic architecture incorporates stone archways and clerestory ceilings. Inside, soaring stained glass, resplendent gold leaf, fabulous Renaissance paintings and numerous marble and bronze sculptures dazzle visitors. The sacrifice required to fund and build it is unimaginable. The ionic LDS Salt Lake Temple is pedestrian by comparison. I don't believe opulence creates holiness, but I'm awed by the devotion of those who did.

We were about to exit the cathedral when an usher directed us to the basement crypt where Australian Cardinal George Pell was laid to rest last week. We descended the stairs and found ourselves almost alone in the silent underground crypt. In the dim lighting, we were taken aback by gorgeous inlaid stone flooring, arched ceilings and sacred art around every corner. The usher had asked us to pray over Cardinal Pell's crypt. In a quiet alcove near the rear of the crypt we found the cardinal and offered our silent prayers.

Before returning to the ship, we visited the fabulous and free Art Gallery of New South Wales. We saw masterpieces by Amedeo Modigliani, Pablo Picasso, Paul Cezanne, Andy Warhol, and Vincent Van Gogh, plus works by dozens of Australian artists. We needed more time.

Take me back to Sydney.

Super Bowl Monday in Hobart, Tasmania

Monday, February 13th

Kickoff for Super Bowl LVII was international dateline-adjusted to 10:30 am Monday the 13th in Hobart, Tasmania. We watched a delayed broadcast of the Super Bowl in our stateroom at 6:00 pm. The game was great, halftime was weird, and the ads were awful. In this part of the world, just three dull ESPN ads, for female kickboxing, ESPN sports trivia and European soccer were repeated over and over. We were unable to fast forward through the ads, but thankfully we muted them.

Hobart is an idyllic gem. The reported population is over 250,000 but it looks like a small fishing village under the hillsides. We docked in Sullivan's Cove, at the end of a long ocean finger. Luckily, the "Bi-annual Australian Wooden Boat Festival" was in Sullivan's Cove today. We walked along the boat docks, through boat builder tents, around the model boat displays, then enjoyed performances by the "Salty Sailor's Chorus" and the marching Hobart Bagpipers.

In the afternoon, we savored spicy tempura mushrooms and crispy fish and chips in the outdoor food court. Christeen slaked her first Pepsi since Jamaica. Poor thing. Polynesia, Tonga and New Zealand do not do Pepsi. After her Pepsi reprise, we walked the docks along dozens of historic wooden boats. They ranged from perfect restorations to rusty patina-encrusted survivors, all decorated in festive seafaring flags. I was a kid in the candy store, but by late afternoon Christeen had seen enough. I offered her another Pepsi, but that wasn't enough.

We (actually I) reluctantly returned to the ship, stopping at one last craft market. Tasmania is known for certain native flora and fauna, most notoriously the endemic Tasmanian devil. The devil is a carnivorous marsupial the size of a small dog. They are ugly, with heavy black fur, large heads, stocky build, a terrific sense of smell, a nasty terrifying screech and fierce ripping jaws. Plus, they stink. They are the kind of pet you would give a child molester. Unfortunately, they are also endangered due to a nearly always fatal infectious facial tumor that first appeared in 1996. We didn't see a Tasmanian devil, but at the market, Christeen purchased a clever jaw-opening devil oven mitt.

As the Zuiderdam sailed toward the setting sun, a flotilla of wooden boats, sails aloft with colors fluttering in the breeze, escorted us out of Sullivan's Cove into the Southern Ocean. What a day.

Off to Adelaide.

Bi-annual Australian Wooden Boat Festival

Happy Valentine's Day

Tuesday, February 14th

Happy Valentine's to Christeen, my patient, lovely and devoted bride of 53 years; to Natalie, Camie, Deidre, Erica and Mindi, my beautiful overachieving daughters; to Madelayne, Emily, Amber, Avery, Breanna, Nicole, Olivia, Penelope and Colette, my brilliantly talented granddaughters; and to Belle, Juliette, Amelia, Olive and Jade, my precious great-granddaughters! These lovely ladies bless me beyond belief. And Happy Valentine's to my five sons-in-law, my nine grandsons, my eight grandsons-in-law, and my great grandson, together with two more great granddaughters due in July. I am the Planned Parenthood poster child.

On the World Stage (as they just re-named the Mainstage) this Valentine's afternoon, Hyperion Knight performed a piano concerto featuring works from Chopin, Bach and Rachmaninoff. He credits his odd given name to his drug-fogged parents from the 1960s in Haight Ashbury. (I think he said they named his sister "Tumbleweed.") Like Elliot Finkel, Hyperion's fingers flew as he delivered Rachmaninoff's insanely difficult *Piano Concerto Nos. 2 and 3*. (Per Hyperion, "Rocky II and III"). On the big screen overhead, his fingers torched the ivories of the big black Steinway. How he does that, or more incredibly, how Rachmaninoff wrote *Concertos 2 and 3*, is a mystery. Hyperion gave us one clue: Rachmaninoff apparently dedicated his *Concerto No. 2* to his shrink. Maybe being slightly off-center helped.

A few weeks ago, Andy Fletcher, a Colorado physicist, presented a series of guest lectures on such timely topics as "Life, the

Universe and Everything," "Gravity and the Big Bang," "Quantum Theory," "Chaos Theory" and other revelatory gems. Most of it was Greek to me, and some was Greek to Andy as well, since he salted his presentations with: "I don't understand this, but...." or "This makes no sense, but...."

During one lecture, he declared the human brain the most miraculous, most complicated and least understood creation in the universe. I agree and I've decided to become a neurologist in my next life, since neurologists know little about neurology, and still make big bucks. Andy pointed out that you cannot dissect a brain and find the file where the ABCs or the Ten Commandments or the Gettysburg Address or Mom's photos are stored. Nor has anyone been able to understand how the brain processes various stimuli controlling our appendages or eyelids or heartbeat or vision or hearing or anything else. The dissected brain is a glob of gray gook providing no clues. All we know is, it's marvelous and incredible. That should make all neurologists True Believers.

According to Andy, the brain comprises 86 billion neurons (who counted them?), which independently and collectively perform neurological functions. But we don't know which neurons do what. Or why sometimes they work together and other times not. Or how they specialize. An important question is, how do we use our 86 billion? Do we slather ourselves on the sofa, order a Big Gulp, click on *Entertainment Tonight* and neutralize our neurons, or do we relentlessly work them? Working neurons must be the talent enablers of Elliot Finkel, Hyperion Knight and Sergi Rachmaninoff. All the great thinkers in human history, the scientists, inventors and philosophers, must have driven their neurons slavishly.

Most of my 86 billion prefer resolute relaxation. Tonight, after Valentine's lobster and filet mignon, we tapped our feet in the Rolling Stone Lounge until the wee hours (about 9:00 pm), then trundled off to bed. Nighty night neurons. Life is good.

Sailing the Southern Ocean

Sunday, February 19th

We're on the Southern Ocean, about midway between Adelaide in South Australia and Perth in Western Australia. The Zuiderdam is lolling at a steady 15 knots like a gigantic porpoise, the bow dipping below the horizon into the oncoming swells, then rising toward the cloudless sky, up and down, up and down. Out on the promenade deck early, I watched the muted sky slumber across the rolling indigo sea. Turning east on my second lap, the sky yawned slightly orange along the horizon. On the following lap, a dart of brilliant orange pierced the sleepy sea top and then gradually ascended until a glorious orange ball sat upon the glittering blue. A passing lady said, "I live for that; it's like we pulled it out of the water!" In a matter of minutes, the ascending sphere transformed from a glowing orange ball into a fiery white celestial furnace.

This morning we attended a non-denominational Sunday devotional. The ship's pastor turned the podium over to a guest pastor, Josh McDowell. McDowell was introduced as a renowned evangelist and "author or co-author of over 150 books." Pastor Josh shared his folksy life story from parental abuse and depression, to conversion to Christianity and calling to the ministry. The congregation empathized, laughed, randomly applauded, sprinkled "amens" and enjoyed good fellowship.

We've also attended a couple of devotionals by Arthur Starr, the on-board rabbi. The first titled, "Rappin' with the Rabbi" and another, "The Book of Genesis, Fact or Fiction." Most attendees were Jewish, although there were some curious Christains. The humorous, self-deprecating rabbi led the discussion in Torah scholarship (Genesis through Deuteronomy). He had good things to say about Christians, albeit they "mistakenly believe Jesus is the Messiah." He struggled with the pronouns in Genesis 1:26, "Let *us* make man in *our* own image, after *our* likeness..." because the God of Judaism is singular. He suggested the pronouns could reflect multiple manifestations of one God. That's a stretch. Because the Jewish Messiah has yet to appear, I got the feeling Rabbi Starr wasn't sure if it would ever happen.

Also this morning, Doug Wheeler, an LDS member from Reston, Virginia, invited us to share the sacrament in his stateroom with his wife, Linda and a handful of others. Last week, I spotted Doug on deck wearing a BYU cap, so I introduced myself, and together we trashed-talked the University of Utah Utes. For this cruise, Doug and Linda selected an inside cabin. They maintain an outside view from the bow camera playing on their stateroom TV. They are attending every LDS temple possible on the cruise. It's difficult to be around such righteous people, but we heathens are doing our best to make them look good.

While in beautiful Adelaide last Wednesday, we visited another fabulous free art museum, The Art Gallery of South Australia. The museum's stately stone facade is fronted by a massive Roman colonnade. Inside the entryway, charming Aussie staffers greeted us at the reception desk. The main galleries displayed wonderful European, American and Australian paintings and sculpture from the 16th century to the present. One highlight was an enormous polished stainless-steel sculpture of Captain James Cook sitting on a plank. I have no idea how stainless is sculpted, but that was a jaw-dropper.

The other galleries featured primarily contemporary crap. One forgettable example: two decapitated and gutted horse carcasses, sewn together back to back, with two butts and four hind legs. One butt was planted on the floor, with hind legs spread wide, while the other butt with legs and hoofs extended, hung from the ceiling. The title: "We Are All Flesh." Don't try to imagine it.

Last Thursday, three folk singers from Adelaide, called "The Beggars," performed on the World Stage. The Beggars include a lead guitar/mandolin/violin player and a standup bass player, plus a female singer who also played rhythm guitar. They started with some humorous Aussie folk songs. Then they launched into some Aussie pop hits from the 60s, including "Georgie Girl" and "I'll Never Find Another You" from The Seekers. The female singer sounded like Mama Cass Elliot. They were surprisingly good, considering they didn't have a drummer.

Captain Cook

Fremantle and Perth

Thursday, February 23rd

During the sail away from Fremantle last night, I felt some sadness. We've spent 16 days sailing around eastern, southern and western Australia. We visited seven cities and towns and met dozens of Aussies. We've seen only a tiny part of the largest island nation in the world, but we loved what we saw. Every Aussie we met was helpful and friendly, with an innately wry sense of humor. Aussie DNA seems happy, charming and funny. More than one took me aside and whispered confidentially, "Love having you here, mate, but please don't tell your friends."

Day before yesterday, we boarded a spotless commuter train for a 30-minute ride from Fremantle to central Perth. A billboard enroute read: "Perth has the climate California wishes for." Indeed, Perth lies about the same latitude south as San Diego lies north. Sister cities on opposite sides of the equator. Outside the Perth train station, I asked a friendly lady pushing two toddlers in a pram for the hop-on-hop-off stop. "Don't bother with that, mate," she said. "Take the free Red Line. That loop covers the most important city sites." And indeed it did. After the Red Line, we walked to the harbor and caught a different bus to the 1000-acre Kings Park and Botanical Garden, one of the largest inner-city parks in the world. It took over twenty minutes to drive through the park. A former New Yorker muttered, "This makes Central Park look like a school playground."

The Fremantle Maritime Museum is located on a former WWII submarine base, which was second in importance to Pearl Harbor in the Pacific Theater. It must be an architect's dream to design a building incorporating maritime elements like waves, sails, hulls and prows. The Maritime Museum looks like the designer was handed a blank check: soaring ceilings, complex curving roof lines, expansive windows and sculpted walls. One museum staffer quipped, "The architect put form ahead of function here, mate." As a result, the spectacular west-facing windows have been blocked, protecting priceless exhibits from searing solar sabotage.

Notwithstanding functional foibles, the building is stunning. Inside, ship models and exhibits of all things maritime, plus *Australia II,* the first Aussie yacht to win the America's Cup and the yacht *Parry Endeavor.* In the *Endeavor*, Aussie Jon Sanders *solo* circumnavigated the world three times (for a total of 658 days) without setting foot on land, or receiving any food, water or supplies. (And we wondered how we'd endure 128 days in a floating amusement park.)

In a shed adjacent to the Maritime Museum, a half dozen retired volunteers mothered over antique marine steam engines. After they regaled us in the history and use of various engines, I asked for directions to the Shipwreck Museum. Volunteer "Jack" said, "Follow me." He led us on a shortcut through a half dozen back alleys. What a guy.

The Shipwreck Museum is a converted 19th-century brick prison built by convicts for convicts. The highlight of the museum is the remains of the Dutch East India merchant ship *Batavia.* Loaded with gold and silver during her maiden voyage, she ran aground on June 4, 1628, near unexplored islands off the coast of Australia. Due to the heavy payload, she rolled and sank on her side. Treasure hunters discovered her in 1972 and found a large portion of the portside hull that had been buried and preserved in coral for 343 years. Excavators removed and restored the timbers and reconstructed the half-hull inside the Maritime Museum. They also salvaged numerous cannons, cannonballs, copper tools, porcelain and buckets of gold and silver coins. The *Batavia* exhibits are surreal, and the story of the aftermath of the sinking is woven with intrigue and horror. More than 200 sailors survived the sinking, but led by a ruthless band of mutineers, only 80 were still alive when rescue ships arrived three months later. In the gift shop, I selected a *Batavia* book. Andrea, an affable dark-haired clerk, frowned slightly, looked side to side and whispered, "If you're interested in the history of *Batavia*, there's a better book. This one takes liberty with the facts." She directed me to a better book at a better price. I thought, "Gotta love these Aussies." Then she told me she was Italian.

The creaking Zuiderdam is battling heavy swells under blustery skies this afternoon. Captain Friso just reported another cyclone days ahead and threatening Madagascar. Perfect conditions for a good shipwreck story.

Fremantle Maritime Museum

Musical Orgy on the Indian Ocean

Friday, February 24th

Besides the terrific Rolling Stone Lounge Band, there are three other musical acts on the Zuiderdam. In the Ocean Bar, The Dance Band is a four-piece jazz ensemble that also does backup for guest entertainers on the World Stage. They are from Toronto, attended a jazz music academy together and were hired by Holland America as a group.

In the Explorer Lounge a pianist and violinist do classical music, Broadway hits and some pop standards. In the Billboard Lounge, two pianists play and sing facing one another on back-to-back Steinways. The evolving Rolling Stone Band now has three lead singers and four instrumentalists: a lead guitarist from the Canary Islands, drummer from Croatia, keyboardist from Rome and bass guitarist from Mexico City. None of the seven had met before being hired by HAL. They're the best cover band I've ever heard, by a *huge* margin.

Last night, The Dance Band did a show on the World Stage called "Jazzed Up Beatles." Following that show all 15 musicians participated in a "Music Walk," where they rotated to the different lounges. The lounges were standing-room-only as these 15 demonstrated wonderful depth and versatility. I saw people wipe away tears as these musicians sang and performed as if they were in Carnegie Hall. Later, the sweet and shy classical violinist joined The Band with a scintillating rendition of Led Zeppelin's "Stairway to Heaven." Following a roaring standing ovation, she quietly said, "I try to live my life for unforgettable moments and this has been one." She thanked the audience and The Band for fulfilling her "secret fantasy" to become a rock star and added, "I'll never forget this night."

At the end of the evening, a lead singer from The Band summed up: "Tonight has been wonderful. Each of us have worked with many musicians over the years, but none of us ever worked with the extraordinary talent on this ship."

I wish my high school band mates could've seen it.

The Dance Band

The Old Man and the Sea

Saturday, February 25th

Glorious sea days! The wind is gentler this morning, kneading the waves under stubbornly overcast skies. Our heading is WNW sailing toward Port Louis, Mauritius at 17 knots. My computer was hot to the touch this morning and the screen read: "error xj8i5gi@tzx3h7*** unable to locate the hard drive." What? Should I look under the bed? I unplugged it, allowed a half hour to cool down, and it restarted.

I've looked forward to this cruise to be able read some classic literature without distraction. Due to luggage weight limits, I only packed three books and Kindled some others. So far, I've read Dicken's *Great Expectations*, Eliot's *Middlemarch* and Melville's *Moby Dick*. Now I'm into Conrad's *Heart of Darkness*, and after that will start *Batavia's Graveyard* by Mike Dash. I have several Kindle downloads to occupy future sea days: *The Complete Works of Shakespeare*, Cervantes' *Don Quixote*, Wolfe's *Look Homeward Angel* and Tolstoy's *War and Peace*. I also packed *Ulysses* by James Joyce, which I hope to finish before reaching Dublin.

Before age 30, I thought 70 was old and over. Most on this ship are 60 and beyond. We're old, but we're not finished. Physical fun is a fading fairy tale. By default, we're on the high road to intellectual stimulation. Conveniently, Holland America continues to provide World Stage "guest lectures" covering timely topics like "Differences Between Spoken and Written Language," "Funnels, Flags and Funny Paint," and "What the Scientists Think About It All." For each lecture, the theater is filled with eager, and intermittently dozing sponges, like me.

Why subject ourselves to such inane trivia? Because we're unable to subject our creaky bodies to pickleball or cornhole or hide-and-go-seek. We're out of shape and misshapen. For many of us, a good day is navigating ship corridors without a face plant. There was a time when fun and games meant *participation* in contact sports. Now it means finding the remote. But as long as we can retain moderate cranial and electronic connectivity, we're happy.

Pass the Twinkies, please.

We're All Here Cause We're Not All There

Tuesday, February 28th

The Zuiderdam is an 11-story personality petri dish. Christeen and I selected the "open seating" dinner option, which means we spin the wheel for dinner dates. Sometimes we win yakity-yakers, or full-of-selfers, or been-everywherers, or some combination of all three. Occasionally we get a silent single sulker, but usually we dine with unassuming folks interested in small talk: "What's your name?" "Where y'all from?" "How'd you meet?" "Is this your first world cruise?" "Do you have any kids?" "Grandkids?" We usually win comparative grandkids one-upmanship.

Some questions we don't ask: "Are you married?" "Have you *never* been married?" "Is this your first marriage?" "How many times *have* you been married?" "Do your kids still live with you?" "What's your favorite medication?" Asking such questions would be rude, and actually unnecessary. People regularly volunteer their pathetic past like sordid survivors: "My ex-husband emotionally abused me for years, beat up the dog, robbed the neighborhood ice cream truck and is now thankfully institutionalized in upstate New York. It took me years to get my life back. And then, (swooning) I met George!"

I popped a brainless question the other night. On a dressy formal evening, we happened upon Captain Friso and his lovely lady in the dining room. Our amiable, approachable Dutch Captain is fortyish, about 6'6", with a Charles Barkley haircut. His lady is about a 6'3" brunette Barbie doll. I roundly greeted the Captain and asked to be introduced to his lovely wife. To which Friso coughed, his lady tossed eye darts, and he mumbled, "This is my, er, girlfriend… " I grimace-grinned and we scurried to our table. I didn't catch Barbie's name.

In the dining room, we can sit at a private table for two, at a table for four, or at a table of eight or even ten. We avoid the big tables, since you can't listen to multiple conversations and get to know all the people anyway. Our preference is a table for four. We dined last week with a couple from New Mexico. He was a retired plaintiff's attorney. Before I'd introduced myself he said, "Don't ever agree to be the trustee of a trust." I assured him I'd never consider such a thing. As trustee, he had just settled his deceased father's estate in San Diego. "It's very stressful," he said. He said he grew up in New York but attended New Mexico State because, "It was the only school that accepted me."

"I'm not very smart," he volunteered matter-of-factly. "I did alright in preparatory school, but only because I studied very hard." He mentioned he retired last December, sold his practice to an associate, and embarked on this world cruise to "decide what to do in retirement." Since he feared he couldn't decide in 128 days, they're staying on the Zuiderdam until the end of July.

I suggested painting as a pastime.

"Way too stressful," he said. "I took a two-hour painting class last fall and got a debilitating backache."

On another recent evening we dined with a mother and her daughter. I'd guess the frail mother was in her early 90s and the rubenesque daughter was in her mid 60s. The talkative daughter boasted she just signed a contract on this ship to buy a house in Atlanta "sight unseen."

"You probably haven't heard of anyone doing that!" she proudly exclaimed.

Probably not.

"I love Atlanta. We're selling Mom's house in Pacific Beach near San Diego and moving to Atlanta where I'll be her caregiver."

To which Mother stammered, "You're not selling my house!"

The daughter smiled exasperatedly. "You signed the papers, Mother."

"What papers? I never signed any papers. You're NOT selling my house! I've lived in my house for forty years and I'm NOT moving!" The daughter leaned across the table, and confidentially said, "She signed the papers, and she knew what she was doing. She changes her mind a lot."   Wink, wink.

"I have NOT signed any papers," Mom said to herself.

The daughter continued in a semi-whisper, "My brother is a bad person. He was the trustee of the family trust. After Dad died, he took $7 million from the trust and bought himself a mansion in Oregon. Now I'm the trustee. Of course, his lawyers are contesting that, but I'm trying to keep Mom away from all that lawyerly nastiness."

"I'm NOT selling my house," Mom repeated.

The daughter rolled her eyes.

I struggled to empathize with both mother and daughter. I smiled at the defiant mother and said to the daughter, "She's fortunate to have you. How's the swordfish?"

We have more than a few eccentrics on board. One elderly lady is fond of unusual hats. She has quite the collection, including a patchwork witch hat, a hat shaped like a strawberry, a tomato hat, a carrot hat and my personal favorite, the cheeseburger hat. Another elderly gal with thinning hair has a large teddy bear she carries everywhere, on and off ship. She not only carries it around, she seats it next to her during shows and converses with it.

"Are you comfortable there, dear? Can you see ok?"

I've never had a conversation with this lady, only a "hello" now and again. My friend Ron has chatted with her, however. He says she's from Florida, is married and appears to have her faculties intact. She says she enjoys cruising alone.

I'd bet her hubby enjoys her cruising alone as well.

Tomato hat

Humor on the High Seas

Wednesday, March 1st

    Whatever happened to funny people like Jack Benny, Bob Hope, Carol Burnett, Jackie Gleason, Joan Rivers, Lucille Ball, Johnny Carson, Jay Leno and Jerry Seinfeld? All except Jay and Jerry are on the highway to heaven. They were hilariously G-rated funny and sadly, many millennials and Gen Xers haven't heard of them. Their art form has been replaced by comedy routines frequented with the F word (as noun, adjective, verb and adverb). Thankfully, comedians on board haven't defaulted to F word humor. However, many have joked about archaic anatomies, dysfunctional body parts and dementia. Christeen and I righteously boycott the "edgy" late shows and instead search our stateroom TV for wholesome R rated movies.

    I'm a comedy curmudgeon. I've intercepted Jimmy Fallon or Steven Colbert while channel surfing. They are pretty good at saying dumb things, but they don't seem very funny. On the other hand, my daughter Erica would think they're hilarious. But Erica loves laughter and could find funny in a celery stick.

    The "Biddys," a trio of thirty-something Irish sisters, appeared as silly old ladies on the World Stage the other night. Of the several comedy shows we've seen so far, the Biddys have been the pottiest. Apparently little old Irish ladies like to share naughty stories and a pint, whilst knitting.

    Here's a couple of PG examples of humor on board:

From the Biddys:

"Sophie dearie, why da ya have that suppository stuck in yer ear?"

"Whatever are ya sayin', Annie? I don'na have no suppository stuck in me ear!"

Annie plucks the waxy missile from Sophie's ear.

"Yes, ya do, and here 'tis!"

"Well, a'll be. Now me knows where me hearin' aid is!"

This one was from Steven Scott, a comedian from NYC:

"Good night, Henry," Mildred says as she closed the lamp.

Presently, Mildred feels a hand on the back of her neck, slowly circling her hairline then dropping across her shoulders, fingers tenderly massaging as they go. The hand gently slides down her back, her breathing quickens. Mildred feels sensations she hasn't felt in years, maybe decades. In the small of her back the hand delicately strokes back and forth, up and down. Mildred tingles, muffles a gasp and squirms slightly. Then the hand stops. Mildred breathlessly sits up, and flicks on the light.

"Henry, why did you stop?!"

Irritated, Henry rolls over and exclaims, "Stop what Mildred?"

"I found the remote."

The other night a singer boasted he had enjoyed wonderful cruises on many Holland America ships, including the Statendam, Oosterdam, Volendam, Zaandam, Amsterdam and Zuiderdam. Then he paused, and said, "Well, I did have an unsavory experience on the Wedontgiveadam."

Missing Madagascar; Magical Mauritius and Reunion

Sunday, March 5th

The weather finally caught up with us. I've been looking forward to Madagascar, but it's not to be. Captain Friso has diverted our course 200 miles south to avoid Cyclone Freddy, presently twisting around the southern tip of Madagascar toward the Mozambique Channel. Seas are heavy and it's windy. The arthritic Zuiderdam creaks in the swells. It could use a few barrels of WD-40 on the seams and joints.

We enjoyed Mauritius and Reunion immensely. I'd heard of Mauritius but had no idea where it was and had never heard of Reunion. Mauritius is famous for the extinct flightless Dodo bird and for expansive coral reefs surrounding super snorkeling spots. Both islands are mountainous and densely populated. They're between 400 and 500 miles east of Madagascar, and each is less than a quarter the size of Jamaica. Mauritius was granted independence from England in 1968, and Reunion is a French territory. Consequently, they drive on the right in Mauritius and on the left in Reunion.

In Mauritius we hired Eimr, a middle-aged Indian taxi driver. He held firm on his "you have me all day" fare. Once underway he proclaimed, "Money not important; important you be happy. You want stop, we stop. I wait for you. I not leave you. You pay on return ship. If you not happy, you pay nothing. If you happy, you pay good tip." Clearly, we were about to be made happy.

A Mauritian native, Eimr's parents were born in India, and he's the youngest of twelve children. Eimr stated over 50% of the Mauritius population is of Indian descent, 30% are African and the remainder are a mix of Chinese, Indonesian and European. Culturally, geographically, religiously and economically, Mauritius is diverse.

A Muslim dressed like a westerner, Emir proclaimed "Muslims can have four wives, but for me, one enough!" The predominant religions on the island are Hindu, Islam and Catholic. We saw no LDS buildings. "We very happy people; always smile. Everyone work. Low tax, hospital free. Low crime, no murder."

Mauritius is one of the world's most densely populated countries, and it seems everyone has a car. In heavy traffic, Eimr drove his Toyota minivan like Mario Andretti with a death wish. Happy Eimr drove "pedal to the metal," always forced his way while merging, never allowed anyone to merge ahead of him and regularly passed with cars/trucks/motorbikes fast approaching in the oncoming lane. Our scary all-day ride included stops at a model ship workshop, a garment factory, a Hindu temple, the Black River Gorges National Park, the Rock Garden, a local market, Le Morne beach and the Port Louis City Center. Most were terribly touristy, surrounded by breathtaking beauty.

Many taxi drivers have become tourism entrepreneurs. They pull out a map, suggest a route and recommend popular attractions, including shopping and restaurants. At certain stops, the drivers may receive a referral fee. Eimr took us to a clothing factory and retail store off the beaten path. Taxis filled the parking lot, and the smartly dressed staff were pros at the hard sell. Caveat emptor: buyer beware of both price and quality. Later Eimr dropped us at a restaurant. "Food very good. Price reasonable," he promised. We invited him to join us, but he humbly declined. The food and prices were ok, not great. After the meal, we found him eating alone at a table outside. He sheepishly admitted the restaurant provides a complimentary meal whenever he delivers customers.

Back in the city center, shimmering afternoon sunlight on storefronts and pedestrians provided perfect photo ops. But Eimr was on his "Mauritius 500" final lap, and getting good still images from the backseat of the flying Toyota was nigh impossible.

At the port, I thanked Eimr and tipped generously. Not because I was overly happy, but because we had arrived alive.

Reunion is characterized by two extinct volcanoes, the largest rising over 10,000 feet, with sugar cane lowlands between the volcanoes and sporadic sandy beaches along the coast. HAL provided a 30-minute shuttle from the port at La Possession north to the coastal community of Saint-Denis. The route included a spectacular new freeway built over the ocean parallel to vertical unstable rock cliffs. Reputedly, it's the most expensive road section in the French empire at a cost of $2.3 billion. No oxymoron: it's a beautiful freeway.

We spent the day walking the streets of Saint-Denis. All tourist brochures, street signs, maps, museum exhibits, park placards and restaurant menus were in French. We tried, but were unable to get any waiter or cashier to translate menus. It reminds me of our last trip to Paris. No Frenchies would translate there, either. Despite the language barrier, we had a lovely time walking past dozens of historic mansions, colorful shops, and another fine botanical garden.

Christeen said she walked over 14,000 steps on the day. I'm trying to catch up.

Let There Be Light

Monday, March 6th

Angry seas this morning, littered with white caps.

I've been listening as fellow cruisers make plans for upcoming ports. I hear about sightseeing or adventure tours, botanical gardens, wildlife preserves, natural history and arts museums or just checking off a bucket list. Most priorities include markets and shopping. The options in every port make a world cruise so entertaining. Unfortunately, with so little time and so many ports, it's difficult to remember where we saw what, when. It's a good thing phone cameras store thousands of dated images.

I've been astonished by the endemic species (species originating) in a given country. Take Mauritius, for example. There are 311 plant species found naturally *only* in Mauritius. Additionally, there are numerous endemic bird and reptile species, including certain bats, pigeons, parakeets, kestrels, starlings, flycatchers, swiftlets, boas, geckos and skinks. Plus an unknown number of *extinct* endemic species, including the famous "dodo" bird. Mauritius is a tiny island in the vast Indian Ocean, yet there are hundreds of species found only on this geographic pinhead.

Even more incredible, Madagascar, (which unfortunately cyclone Freddy nixed for us), has more than 11,000 endemic plant species, plus hundreds of endemic mammals and reptiles. In fact, scientists estimate about 90% of the plants and 85% of the animals found on Madagascar are endemic. On top of that, Madagascar is home to 100,000 endemic species of insects. (And we think house flies are a nuisance.) It's a shame Freddy cost us a visit to that creative wonderland.

Seeing rare natural flora and fauna in the delicious light of the Southern Hemisphere is heavenly. In the summer of 2004, three friends and I rode motorcycles to the Arctic Circle. We called our little adventure "Chasing the Sun" because we were following long summer daylight in the Northern Hemisphere. When we arrived at the Arctic Circle, the sun set after midnight and then took only a short nap on the horizon before introducing another day.

Photographers and painters are obsessed with light. Early morning and late afternoon sunlight deepens both hue and shadow, producing vivid changes in color, depth and contrast. We romanticize sunrises and sunsets because of dramatic atmospheric color changes. Without light, there is no color; there is no shape. In the absence of light, there is nothing. The source, angle and intensity of light produce the color.

The Christian gospel has been defined as "truth," and truth is defined as "light." God embodies all truth, therefore by definition God is light. We've heard hell is a place of "fire and brimstone." That's not possible, since fire makes light and there is no light in hell. Hell must be completely devoid of light; an eternal blackout.

Light makes nature beautiful. The more of nature we see, the more astonished we are at the beauty and mystery of creation. After reading *Moby Dick* again, I wonder why God created a 400,000-pound warm-blooded mammal with lungs, unable to breathe underwater, half again as large as a tractor trailer rig and then put it deep in the ocean, amongst a gazillion varieties of cold-blooded gill breathers? I wonder why He created awkward hopping marsupials with tiny forelegs and elongated hind legs; the mothers of which birth a fetus, which instinctively belays up mom's belly into a pouch, remaining for up to two years until it can hop out on its own? God had a perfectly good template for quadrupeds. Why create something so strange? Or how did He come up with transparent lizards? Or insanely chromatic parrots and geckos. Or koala bears that eat *only* eucalyptus leaves? Or dromedaries that can slog through 100 miles of hot sand across an arid desert without a drink? Or ordinary cattle that convert prairie grass to filet mignon? So much of creation is so gloriously bizarre.

Did God create all to prove that nothing is impossible? How about parking those 11,000 plant species only on Madagascar? Are the soils and climate in Madagascar so unique that it's the only place in the world where such species can survive and thrive? Hardly. Madagascar is a mere 250 miles from the African continent. So why did He do it that way? In the next life I'm enrolling in Fundamentals of Creation, Origins of the Universe and Species Selection. I've got a load of questions for the academic angels.

Which brings me back to light. Another definition for light is inspiration. To become enlightened is to learn something. We'll never learn all the mysteries of the world and of creation, but we can seek "the light" to understand more than we know. Traveling the world is enlightening; reason enough to be on every bucket list.

Maputo farmer's market

Maputo, Mozambique

Wednesday, March 8th

Mozambique is one of the poorest countries in the world. Annual GDP per capita in 2022 was $581. In 2022, about 21 million of its 33 million people suffered "extreme poverty," which is defined as living on $1.90 *per day*. That's $1.90 for food, water, clothing, shelter, transportation, utilities, medicine, and entertainment. Maputo is the capital city with over a million residents and Mozambique's most important commercial port. This morning hazy skies blanket a chalky Maputo landscape filled with older mid-rise buildings and barking traffic. There are some shiny new buildings, but the city skyline is convincingly third-world.

At sea last week, cruise director Ian spoke fondly of our weeks in French Polynesia and the South Pacific then added, "Now we're going to Africa for a month. Be prepared, it's very different." He repeatedly cautioned about crime in major African cities: "Leave jewelry and expensive watches aboard, walk in groups, avoid walking in questionable areas, secure wallets and purses and be aware of surroundings at all times." Additionally, "No picture-taking of government buildings or uniformed officers and be wary of shady taxi operators. Always agree to the fare in writing before taking a taxi. Avoid taxi drivers who do not speak English."

This morning we joined the HAL excursion, "Sights of Maputo." The tour description included the African experience: "Tour guides may not speak English. Tour guides may not be properly trained. Tour buses may not be clean or regularly maintained or air conditioned. Roads may be pot-holed and rutted, and walkways may be unsafe."

Having thus been warned, we were surprised to board a sparkling clean bus with excellent air-conditioning and a helpful tour guide who spoke fluent English. The tour included a half-dozen popular tourist sites: the Maputo Fortress, the historic Maputo Railway Station, Independence Square and the Steel House designed by Gustave Eiffel. Unfortunately, Eiffel never visited Mozambique and had no idea how impractical a steel two-story house would be in sweltering southern Africa. We also visited the Museum of Natural History, an expansive farmer's market and a lively crafts market.

At every stop we were swarmed by sweaty street merchants peddling Mozambique t-shirts, ball caps, jewelry, art, woodwork, leatherwork, mangos, cashews and more. We'd smile and say, "No, obrigado." (Portuguese is the official language of Mozambique, but every seller spoke enough English.) Step away and the stalking seller would drop the price and amp the pressure: "I give you two for one. I make you great price, my friend. You don't want, then buy for gift!"

It became annoying. I tried to look each person in the eye, and when I did, the eyes plead, "Buy something from me!" I wanted to take photos of those expressive faces, but it would've been demeaning. I wanted to give them all a few dollars and say, "Please keep your stuff."

Certainly, Maputo street vendors aren't living on $1.90 a day, but they can't be making much. Worse off were people languishing in the shade on sidewalks and cluttered street corners. A streetscape characterized by dust, dilapidated buildings, battered vehicles and prolific potholes. But we also saw a few BMWs and Mercedes, and the winding coastal route back to the ship was lined with oceanfront residences similar to La Jolla shores. Our tour itinerary didn't include any of the 21 million subsisting on $1.90 a day. No tour provided that.

The future of Mozambique is sketchy. Huge untapped natural gas reserves lie offshore within Mozambique territorial waters. Development of such reserves could provide an economic windfall for the entire country. But realization of that economic tsunami is clouded by the reality of chronic corruption and political instability, including a militant Islamic insurgency that has been raging since 2017 in the northern Cabo Delgado Province.

In the crowded farmer's market, we bought a hand-packed pound of crispy roasted and salted cashews. Later, as we boarded the bus at Independence Square, a skinny street hawker walked outside the bus, pounding the windows and holding a plastic pack of cashews in his sweaty palm, eyes pleading. I couldn't resist and motioned him to the bus door. I bought a sweaty package. I put the package in Christeen's lap and said, "Have some cashews."

"I'm not eating those," she said.

Turns out the street seller's cashews were as fresh and crisp as the farmer's market cashews. Both were delicious, with a smoky roasted flavor. I doubt I'll remember much about the touristy sites of Maputo. But as I walked back to the port, fingering the few useless dollars still littering my pockets, I couldn't forget all the pleading eyes.

"Welcome to Durban" sand sculpture

Durban Drive By and East London Eclipse

Saturday, March 11th

We got a taste of the African experience in Durban, South Africa yesterday. After completing the South African Immigration Service's passport "face-check," we shuttled into the Durban city center. The buses were full-sized and not ancient, but well-worn and generally grimy. The shuttle dropped us near an aquatic park called Ushaka Marine World. The park, which hadn't opened for the day, was at the opposite end of an outdoor seaside shopping center a la Seaport Village in San Diego. The shops were lined along both sides of a single colorful corridor, with a central plaza leading to the aquatic park and beach. We purchased a few items in a sweltering shop and then proceeded to the beach.

The cool beach breezes were instantly refreshing. Low tide and moist hard pack made walking easy along a wide swath of white sand. Ahead of the tide line, the deep white sand was littered with random broken seashells and tidal debris. I paid "Ken," a local sand sculptor, $2.00 for a photo of Christeen beside his "Welcome to Durban" creation.

We returned to the ship for an afternoon HAL excursion. On the return shuttle, moisture dripped from an air conditioning vent above an empty seat. The dripping continued until the driver applied the brakes, then the vent gushed yellow liquid. Meanwhile, we baked inside the bus. Mercifully, the ride was short.

The interior of our "Panoramic Durban" excursion bus was slightly less dingy; however, many of the seat backs were stuck in the semi-reclining position. A plastic porta-potty crudely marked "For Urination Only" stood inside the rear door. Our cheery Afrikaner tour guide cautioned us against drinking anything unless "absolutely necessary," as there were no scheduled restroom stops. We wisely thirsted it out and avoided the in-bus amenity. During the drive he entertained us with Durban and South African history, politics, family lore and trivia. But with engine noise, the scratchy sound system, and his Afrikaner accent, we missed much of it.

"Panoramic Durban" was more accurately "Panoramic Cane Fields and Coastline." We enjoyed the long drive up the coast but made only two stops: Tongaat Beach South and Tongaat Beach North, aka Finney's Rock. These singular sites, renowned for rip currents and sea foam spray, were just a quarter mile apart. Both required navigating steep rocky steps to the shoreline and neither was particularly impressive. The short road from the main highway to Tongaat was lined with impressive ocean view homes protected by cameras, perimeter walls, iron gates and security guards. I'd rather have seen more of Durban, both the city and the port. On our return, we did see a bit more of the gritty city center, but heavy traffic and our guide's desire to be on time prompted a disappointing shortcut through town.

South Africa has a significant auto manufacturing industry and many other worldwide manufacturers have a presence here. There are hundreds of new cars and trucks, both import and export, parked dockside in Durban. Dozens of new John Deere tractors and combines, together with Volvo heavy-mining trucks, cranes and other industrial equipment line the docks. The expansive port handles cargo ships, oil tankers, container ships, car haulers and cruise ships. Cranes load and unload around the clock. Just beyond the harbor, dozens of shipping vessels are queued, awaiting a dock vacancy. For me, a dockside tour would've been far more interesting than sea spray and security guarded homes at Tongaat Beach.

Commercial vessels, including cruise ships, are required to hire local pilots to navigate the shoals, currents and ocean depths in each port of call. The ship's captain and navigator step aside as a local pilot assumes control during harbor transit and docking. Occasionally, heavy seas prohibit the pilot from safely boarding a ship from the pilot boat. In that case, either the ship misses the port or the pilot is transported by helicopter to and from the ship. Last night in windy conditions, a hovering helicopter dropped a cable to the local pilot standing on the top deck aft. He clipped the cable to his body harness and the chopper whisked him off ship.

Captain Friso just announced he has aborted the attempt to dock at East London. It's very windy and Friso warned us yesterday he was "not optimistic" the weather would allow us to dock. He said this is the largest ship to attempt docking at East London. The dock and harbor are relatively small, and successful docking would've required an expert local pilot, together with near-perfect weather conditions. We had the pilot on board, but the weather didn't cooperate. (HAL had originally scheduled a smaller Rotterdam class vessel for this world cruise but later switched to the larger Vista class Zuiderdam. I subsequently overheard a ship's officer remark that the Zuiderdam had no chance of docking at East London, regardless of the weather.)

I took some photos of the East London skyline, and that's as close as we got. It's a bummer, as we had booked an excursion to the Inkwenkwezi Private Game Reserve. We're going to miss seeing some game reserve big kitties.

Doggone it.

Township "petunias"

Three Faces of Port Elizabeth
aka Gqeberha aka P.E.

Monday, March 13th

Port Elizabeth is a South African lady with multiple personalities. It's the most populous city in the Eastern Cape, with urban area population at nearly 1.3 million in 2022. (In the Western Cape, the most populous city is Cape Town). In 1820 Port Elizabeth was named after the deceased wife of governor Sir Rufane Donkin. That historic name was changed in 2021 to Gqeberha which, in Xhosa tribal dialect, is the name of a river near the city. Unfortunately, unless you speak Xhosa, which requires sharp tongue clicking, (like a leather strap smacking a tabletop), the new name is neither pronounceable nor understandable. Predictably, few use it. A local resident commented on this and similar absurdities: "Our politicians are quite good at approving name changes, but rather inept at pothole repair, trash cleanup, crime control, water service, sewage disposal and reliable electricity."

I didn't know California exported politicians to South Africa.

From the ship's terminal, Port Elizabeth looked like a drab metro mural painted above a sooty train station. Mongrezi, our "Tour of the Townships" guide, proudly recited some verse in his native Xhosa. It sounded like a cap gun popping over unintelligible mumbling. He tried, but failed to teach us the Xhosa tongue click. He said windy P.E. was once known as the "Friendly City," but unabated crime has decimated downtown businesses and driven tourists away. The city is dirty, with trash and graffiti all around. Many storefronts are boarded and vandalized, displaying weathered "To Let" signs. Passenger trains once connected P.E. to Cape Town, but with increasing crime they became unsafe, and service was discontinued.

Leaving the city center, we drove past tired schools and government buildings, gritty car repair shops, tire stores, building suppliers and contractor yards. Most businesses had razor wire along fence tops and bars over doors and windows. Graffiti decorated the walls and fences, and trash from plastic bags ripped apart by roving dogs, swirled in the streets. Mongrezi apologized for the trash, explaining that "trash is collected only once a week." Seems once a day wouldn't be enough.

P.E. is the proud hometown of Nelson Mandela, the former Prime Minister elected after the end of apartheid. One Mandela legacy is "township" housing for masses of urban poor. Mandela's program was called the Reconstruction and Development Programme (RDP). Mongrezi called the RDP houses "Mandela houses." They are tiny, about 40 square meters (430sf), with electricity and indoor plumbing built on postage-stamp lots along paved or dirt streets. Two or more families typically occupy each RDP house. Since 1994, more than 5 million RDP houses have been built across South Africa, providing housing for more than 20 million. Mongrezi estimated 600,000 such houses have been built in P. E.

We drove through several townships. There are no lawns or gardens in the poorer townships, but there's so much trash that Mongrezi called the colorful garbage, "township petunias." There's also "middle-class" housing in some townships. A middle-class house is slightly larger than a RDP house, typically with paved streets in the neighborhood and some sidewalks. Mongrezi lives in one of the townships and kindly directed our driver past his middle-class house. It was surrounded by an irregular block fence, with a neighbor's broken-down taxi parked inside. His house would be considered a tear-down in one of Salt Lake City's poorer neighborhoods. But township residents are the fortunate ones. The waiting list for a RDP house is long, qualifications are restrictive, the process is bureaucratic, likely corrupt and new houses are in short supply.

Outside the townships, hundreds of thousands live "settlements" consisting of sprawling adjoining shacks in vacant trashy fields with no electricity, running water or sewer. Water is obtained from a community spigot and must be boiled. Toilets are buckets dumped in community containers, which are emptied once a week. Mongrezi pointed to a cluster of several hundred shacks in a dry riverbed. "During our last torrential rain, shacks in that riverbed were destroyed in the flood. The people lost everything, but because of the disaster, they all received a RDP house. As soon as the river dried up, people built more shacks in the riverbed, praying that another flood would entitle them to a house."

After our sobering township tour, we boarded a HAL shuttle to a "safe shopping center" on the opposite side of Port Elizabeth. Within 20 minutes, we had entered a completely different world. The streets were clean and the landscaped buildings sparkled in the afternoon sun. White sand beaches and resort hotels lined the waterfront. The bus stopped at an enormous, enclosed shopping mall. The parking lot was filled with late-model cars. After our morning tour of the dingy city center, trashy townships and dire settlements, it was like being transported to Newport Beach heaven.

Multiple-personality Port Elizabeth defies description.

Apartheid

Thursday, March 16th

    Apartheid was a system of racial segregation in South Africa enforced by the dominant White minority from 1948 until 1991. Racial discrimination existed in South Africa before apartheid, however egregious laws denying voting rights, prohibiting mixed marriages and requiring relocation of Black families from prime neighborhoods to outlying Blacks-only settlements cemented segregation. Those measures, and others requiring segregation of schools, churches, businesses, transportation and all public places, ensured Blacks had no voice and no rights in South Africa. It took years of indignation and condemnation by the United Nations, together with arms embargoes and economic sanctions, to force change in South Africa. During the 1980s international outrage prompted repeated violent Black demonstrations, accompanied by militant crackdowns by the minority White government, leaving thousands dead or incarcerated. Finally in 1990, under international pressure and opposition from his own party, Prime Minister F. W. de Klerk unconditionally released the anti-apartheid leader Nelson Mandela from prison after *27 years* of incarceration. In April 1994, free elections were held with Blacks finally having the right to vote and Nelson Mandela was elected prime minister.

    Troubling and persistent inequality, the effects of 50 years of apartheid rule, continues throughout South Africa today. More than half of the total population of 60 million live in poverty, with 18 million experiencing "absolute poverty" (less than $1.90 per day). The unconscionable treatment of Blacks is a sordid blight on the history of

South Africa. It's also a blight on the history of humankind, from 17th-century European slave traders to slave owners in the American deep south to discrimination and segregation in 20th-century America. That also applies to the treatment of Native Americans and Native Canadians by White settlers and to the treatment of aboriginals in Australia and similar indigenous peoples everywhere. We may attempt to understand the discriminating behavior of "educated" European explorers and White settlers upon discovery of illiterate indigenous peoples on far away continents. But we're not able to justify it. God does not discriminate. Thank heaven for the likes of Abraham Lincoln in America, and F. W. de Klerk in South Africa, who courageously dismantled decades of oppression in the midst of brutal conflicts and enormous political opposition. In hindsight, why did it take so long? Sadly, even the LDS church, which should have been a "beacon on the hill" for equality, discriminated against Black males by withholding the priesthood until President Spencer W. Kimball was inspired to end that practice in 1978.

Unfortunately, discrimination, racism and inequality continue throughout the world today, despite well-intended efforts by governments, universities, churches and other organizations to eradicate it. In South Africa, after his election in 1994, Nelson Mandela did not seek retribution or revenge for the 27 years he lost in prison. Rather, he taught forgiveness and reconciliation among racial groups. He formed a broad coalition government that approved a new constitution and worked to bring the country together. Unfortunately, he declined a second term, and his successors have been unable to solve the problems of high unemployment, pervasive corruption and punishing poverty.

We may never overcome the effects of man's inhumanity to man. It would take universal forgiveness and forgetting. Not likely to happen given that we humans are still greedy, selfish, judgmental and otherwise fundamentally flawed. Individually however, there's a solution. To live God's great commandment: Love one another.

It's a tall order.

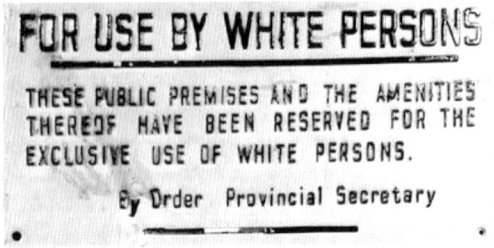

Nelson Mandela cell

Cape Town Conundrum

Thursday, March 16th

Cape Town is a fabulously beautiful slumbering train wreck. We spent two days in port and saw both the unbelievable and the unforgettable. Cape Town lies on the west coast of South Africa at the end of Table Bay under the backdrop of Table Mountain. South of Cape Town an arbitrary, invisible line at the end of Cape Point divides the Atlantic Ocean from the Indian Ocean. The setting of Cape Town has to be seen to be believed. Only the Creator could have sculpted such natural magnificence. I'm surprised Charles Darwin, during his 1836 voyage on the *HMS Beagle,* didn't get religion the instant he saw the place. The harbor, the waterfront and the city center are gleaming gorgeous. No surprise it's considered one of the most artistically beautiful cities in the world. But thanks to the lingering effects of apartheid, the sparkling Cape Town waterfront and glossy city center mask a troubling reality for the teeming millions living just beyond view in poverty.

According to lecturer Daniel Silke, business consultant, Cape Town resident, the pathetic legacy of apartheid lingers on. Silke provided some startling statistics: South African unemployment is currently around 33%. But add the nearly 10% who have given up looking for work and unemployment rises to 42%. The unemployment rate for those aged 15 to 20 is over 60%. In Cape Town, half the population lives in poverty. Less than 3 million of the 60 million South Africans pay 97% of personal income taxes. Because the great majority pay little or no taxes, the government leans socialist, typically resulting in the over-regulation and penalization of private enterprise. The government-owned and operated electric power grid experiences daily power outages due to poor maintenance, lack of capital investment and corruption. At Silke's home, blackouts range from 4 to 8 hours, *daily*. And while school attendance is mandatory, of the 750,000 students who dropped out of school during the pandemic, most have not returned. School attendance is the lowest in 20 years.

Possibly the most worrisome problem is the government culture of corruption. The moral high bar set by Nelson Mandela appears to have been abandoned by his successors. Former Prime Minister Jacob Zuma is accused of bilking the country of billions through bribery, kickbacks and favoritism. Silke reported that widespread corruption continues to pollute the criminal justice system, government services, economic development and politics at every level.

While walking in downtown Cape Town today, Ron and Valentina, our friends from Hurricane, Utah, were approached by five friendly uniformed police officers who stole their credit card. Our friends immediately returned to ship and called to cancel the card. By the time they made the call, the thieves had attempted to make a $9,000 purchase.

Unless the South African government can right itself, obliterate corruption, and provide economic opportunity for all, a day of reckoning will surely come. No country can expect a tiny minority to fund an expensive and crippling socialist agenda forever. Hopefully the political leaders will return to the Mandela example and restore governmental integrity before a national social and economic train wreck is unavoidable.

On our first day in Cape Town, we boarded a ferry to the infamous Robben Island penitentiary, where Nelson Mandela spent 17 of his 27 years behind bars. Our tour guide was an informative gent who had also spent five and a half years incarcerated at Robben Island. We visited Mandela's cell, a tiny 8'x7' cubicle with a concrete floor, a barred window, no bed and no wash basin. The furnishings consisted of a straw floor mat, footstool, tin cup and tin plate. It's impossible to imagine how anyone could spend 17 years in that cell without going bonkers. Remarkably, upon his release, Mandela sought no retribution of any sort against his captors. His is an unparalleled story of mistreatment and suffering followed by complete forgiveness. In life, Nelson Mandela punched his ticket to heaven.

In the afternoon, we toured another township and settlement area. The township was similar to those in Port Elizabeth, but the settlement was different in one respect. The shanties had low-lying electrical cables running along the roofs, with a satellite dish atop almost every shanty. I didn't see any meters, so I presume the electric company looks askance at what might be pirated service. Maybe it's no big deal as the amount of pirated juice to power a TV or phone charger, even in hundreds of shanties, would be relatively insignificant.

Our tour included a stop for lunch at a restaurant inside a township home. As there is no parking on narrow township streets, the bus dropped us a half block away. We were greeted by the tiny 93-year-old proprietor in an African headdress who welcomed us to her home. She acquired the home in 1960 and over the years also acquired the adjacent house, then combined the two into a home restaurant. After relating her life story, she and three assistants served an African buffet consisting of at least 20 mystery dishes and white rice. I took a sample from every dish and loaded my plate. Everything was delicious. What an experience.

During our second Cape Town day, we attempted to ride the cable car to the top of Table Mountain. Unfortunately, gale force winds, together with a fog blanket atop the mountain ("tablecloth" to the locals), shuttered the cable car operation. Alternatively, we took a bus to the top of Signal Mountain for some great city views in the buffeting gale. Later in the day we rode a bus around town, past Ferrari, Aston Martin and Porsche dealerships, to a vibrant, classy multilevel waterfront shopping mall. All of which was completely incongruous with everything we had seen the day before.

Welcome to unbelievable and unforgettable Cape Town, South Africa.

"Tablecloth" over Table Mountain

Namibia: A Different Poverty Picture

Sunday, March 19th

Namibia lies just north of South Africa on the Atlantic coast. It's 20% larger than the state of Texas, has nearly 1,000 miles of coastline, and is one of the least densely populated countries in the world (about 8 people per square mile). It's also still relatively poor, with a per capita annual income in 2022 of $4,358. Namibia has little rainfall and is characterized by the arid Namib and Kalahari deserts, which are separated by a central plateau. The country is so dry only 1% of the land area is arable, and only one tenth of 1% is covered by water.

We spent a day at Luderitz on the south coast, and the following day we docked at Walvis Bay on the central coast. The view from the ship anchored in Luderitz Harbour was a sandy pastel moonscape with a pattering of buildings. Walvis Bay looked similar, but with a ship's terminal and more commercial buildings. Trees are rare along the south-central Namibian coast and grass is practically non-existent. Wind-swept sand dunes rise high along the coastline and extend for up to 100 miles inland.

Luderitz was a sleepy coastal hamlet until 1908, when a diamond was discovered sparkling in the sand. European miners rushed in, but by 1928 the diamond frenzy had shifted to South Africa. Luderitz gradually drifted back into the sands. Today revitalization is underway, with a Waterfront Project that was approved in 2000 and ongoing efforts to save historic buildings. Despite that, quiet Luderitz had a ghost town in the making vibe during our walkabout.

We stepped off the gangway at the Walvis Bay dock onto a

blanket of moist seagull poop. Apparently the locals, only 48% of whom are employed, do not understand that tourists aren't charmed by smelly seagull crap. Our buses were parked at the opposite end of a 300-foot-long dock. As we slathered through the mess in our sneakers, I avoided eye contact with fellow adventurers wearing flip flops. (Thankfully, by the time we returned, the dock had been swept down...by the Zuiderdam maintenance crew.)

We headed 35 kilometers north to Swakopmund (Swakop), a lovely coastal resort town with an area population of about 60,000, the majority of whom live in township and settlement poverty. Our Namibian guide drove us through the township he grew up in. While township and settlement housing here looked similar to that in Port Elizabeth and Cape Town, there were significant differences: In Swakop, no trash anywhere, and no graffiti or razor wire. We repeatedly saw people sweeping and raking the dirt streets. About crime in the settlements, our guide said there is low crime, "Because poor people have little and they look out for one another." Here there are no electric lines or satellite dishes atop shanties. At night people use candles or battery lamps because oil lamps are a fire hazard. If a fire starts in a settlement, the settlement quickly vaporizes.

We made stops at two homes in the townships and one in the settlements. As we passed people on the streets, young and old smiled and waved. At each stop, the people were kind and welcoming. Our guide translated the native dialect of a 72-year-old grandmother wearing a colorful dress and headdress as she described her tribal culture. At a second stop, a matron described herbal medicines and potions next to her plywood and tin roof shack. We were able to smell and touch dozens of natural remedies, everything from aphrodisiac root to rheumatoid-curing baboon poop. She also passed around a jar of rhino poop, but I can't recall its magical properties.

At each stop, neighborhood children and some adults lingered around, the kids shyly grinning and the adults passively curious. I didn't pay much attention to the medicinal qualities of roots and poop, as the beautiful kids were so endearing. One little guy watched us intently as he clutched a toy car in his hand. Another toddler twirled the handle of a white plastic spoon in his mouth as he sternly looked me over. Skinny pre-teen girls in pigtails and dreadlocks giggled and chased one another around the shanties. Three young boys rolled old car and truck tires down the dirt street.

What about their future? Happily, education is free in Namibia, and most parents take education seriously. The Namibian literacy rate is over 80%, and about 97% of the population is Christian. Plus, the government is more stable and less corrupt than in many African nations. Namibia is blessed with diamond, uranium and gold and silver resources, plus a growing tourism industry, a steady agricultural base, 300 sunny days a year and 1,000 miles of oceanfront property. Plus, there's no trash anywhere. In Namibia, it seems the youngsters have at least some chance of escaping the poverty cycle.

At our final township stop, we were treated to an African snack. We washed our hands in the same dirty dishwater bowl and dried them on the same damp towel. Four plates were placed before us. One contained a whitish-gray clump that looked like soiled cornmeal. Another, with a pile of African spinach. The third had baked caterpillars and the fourth contained a watery, hummus-like bean dip. We were instructed to take a clump of the cornmeal between our fingers and sample it with spinach or caterpillars or bean dip, according to our pleasure. The clump tasted like bland cornmeal, the spinach tasted like spinach seasoned with sand, the caterpillars tasted like crunchy chicken skins seasoned with sand, and the watery hummus dip was tasteless. Thankfully, we washed it all down with ice cold Coca-Cola. The taste that refreshes.

Namibia postscript: I am unsure if soiled cornmeal, sandy spinach, baked caterpillars, watery hummus, dirty dishwater, dried baboon and rhino poop, or some combination of all, was to blame for a subsequent ship-wide severe gastric intestinal disorder. In Idaho, we call it the "Rocky Mountain Quickstep." On the Zuiderdam, it was more like the "Ocean Runs Through It." In any event, it rapidly became a gastric tsunami. New food service cleanliness standards were immediately implemented, requiring hand washing upon entering the dining area. Self-service was eliminated for drinks, rolls, fruits, cereal and dessert. Guests were not allowed to touch anything until it appeared on their plates. It took a couple of weeks to run its course (sorry), but we all survived.

Herbal medicines

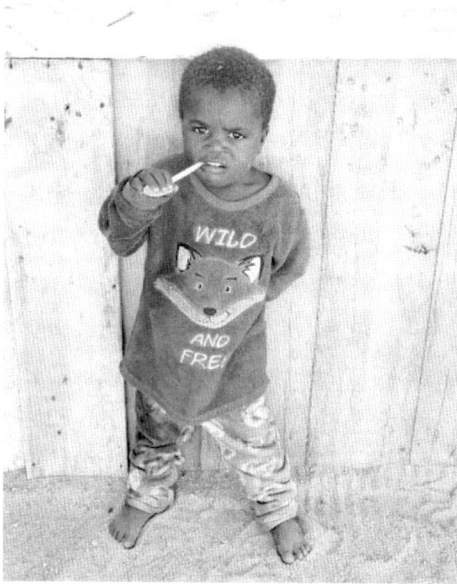

Namibia children

Atlantic African Safari

Monday, March 20th

The seas are calm this hot and humid afternoon under mostly sunny skies. This morning I watched schools of dolphins cavorting around the ship. We are cruising the Atlantic at a moderate 16 knots following the west coast of Africa toward Luanda, Angola. In a few days, we'll cross the equator again. On deck it feels like I'm walking through misters inside a toaster oven, or sweating in a sauna. I've never understood a sauna. Why would anyone pay to sweat? Just move to Florida.

If you were around in the 80s and 90s, you probably recall evening news videos of the raging Angola civil war. It lasted about 27 years and cost an estimated 500,000 lives. In the years since, Angola has struggled to rebuild the resulting devastation and unite a deeply divided populace. The country has rich petroleum and mineral reserves, and Luanda, the capital city with a metro area population of 9 million, is considered the world's most expensive city. We've been tactfully advised not to venture out on our own in Luanda and to leave handbags and jewelry aboard ship.

Angola is nearly twice the size of Texas. It's difficult to grasp the geographic magnitude of the African continent. I did some flight checking, and it takes about 9 hours to fly direct from Cape Town in the south to Tunis, Tunisia in the north. However, an average one-stop flight takes closer to 20 hours. Wanna drive instead? My GPS indicates the shortest route is over 6700 miles, and the estimated driving time is about 150 hours. (Not counting potty breaks, of course.) The African continent is so large that Daniel Silke, the consultant from Cape Town, put an

Africa map on the big screen and placed the following *inside* it: continental United States, Portugal, Spain, Belgium, Netherlands, France, Germany, Switzerland, Italy, all of Eastern Europe, India, Japan and China. For good measure, he also pasted most of the United Kingdom inside Madagascar.

We are on a sea safari with multiple West African ports ahead:

Luanda, Angola

Takoradi, Ghana

Abidjan, Ivory Coast

Banjul, Gambia

Dakar, Senegal

Santa Cruz and Arrecife, Canary Islands

Agadir, Casablanca

Tangier, Morocco

I'm looking forward to all of it. Once beyond Africa, I'm getting anxious to swap my equatorial shorts for some Norwegian woolens.

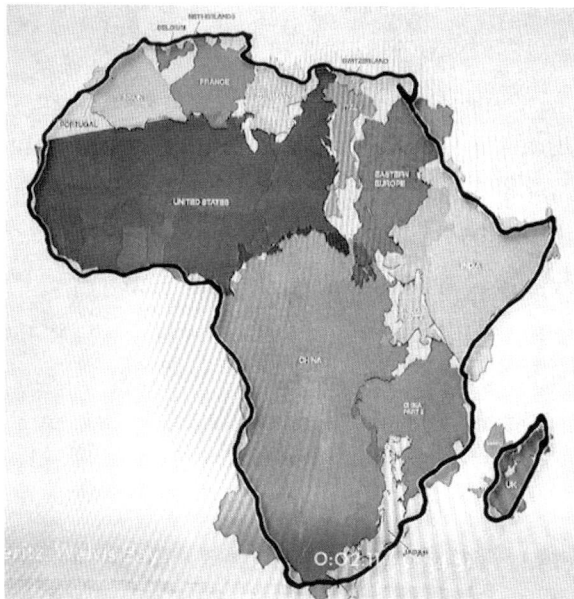

Inequality in Luanda, Angola and the Blind Eye

Wednesday, March 22nd

Luanda, Angola may be the most expensive city in the world, but you'd never guess by appearances. The metro area is characterized by sooty skies above a clanging ships harbor, a massive oil refinery, clotheslines strung across dilapidated apartment buildings, bullet-pocked office buildings, abandoned and active construction projects and depressing shanty slums called "musseques." Luanda is expensive because of high tariffs. A two bedroom apartment in the city rents for an average of $6800 per month. The tariffs were imposed to encourage economic diversity from oil dependency. But Luanda is still expanding oil refining capacity. High prices affect everyone, but have a profoundly crushing impact on the poor, many of whom moved to Luanda seeking safety during the brutal civil war. The city has been overwhelmed by massive in-migration; over half of the area population live in poverty with the city unable to provide reliable basic services.

We joined dozens of others in several mid-sized buses for a tour of Luanda under police escort. Like a funeral cortege, the buses followed a motorcycle cop single file from stop to stop. Jessica, our 26-year-old Angolan tour guide, said she has no car and no other job. So far this year, she's guided just four part-day tours, income from which supports her mother and a brother. We drove past absurdly opulent government buildings and stopped at another Gustav Eiffel iron house, the circa 17th-century Luanda Cathedral, the well-preserved 16th-century Sao Miguel Fortress and the Neto Mausoleum. We encountered lovely people on the streets of the city, but our route carefully avoided the blighted slums, which were visible in the distance anyway.

The most impressive structures in Luanda are the embarrassingly fabulous government buildings and monuments, including the National Assembly of Angola, the Presidential Palace and the Agostinho Neto Mausoleum. Neto was the first president and "founding father" after Angola became independent of Portugal 1975. The government buildings are surrounded by crisply uniformed guards packing over the shoulder automatic rifles. Such largess in a city incapable of providing reliable electricity, clean drinking water and basic sanitation to resident millions seems absurd. The Neto Mausoleum houses Neto's casket for public viewing and looks like a concrete missile rising almost 400 feet over the Luanda skyline. The mausoleum is surrounded by a 4.6 square-mile park and cultural center. It was estimated to cost $40 million and may have been either partially or entirely funded by North Korea. We were permitted inside the mausoleum but we were not permitted to take photos.

Remember the rich man who, having kept every commandment since his youth, took a knee and asked Jesus what he needed to do to get to heaven? Jesus told him to sell everything and "give to the poor." The poor face daunting survival obstacles. And the rich face different daunting obstacles. "Wo unto the rich who refuse to feed and clothe the weary and the poor." Of the rich men casting gifts into the treasury, He said, "For all these have cast of their abundance." But of the widow who cast only two mites, or "all the living that she had," He said, "This poor widow cast in more than they all."

Luanda makes you think. The slums of Africa make you think. Human suffering is everywhere, and the natural inclination is to cast a blind eye. Some fellow passengers stayed aboard in certain African ports because they'd "already seen slums." The sensory African experiences of otherworldly flora, wonderous indigenous wildlife, sculpted deserts and glorious, expansive horizons are all inspiring. We should visit Africa for that. But also to meet lovely people living peaceable, thankful lives in punishing poverty. People in shanty slums, who pray daily for adequate food and clean water, fall in love, get married, have babies, raise families, send kids to school, chat with neighbors, care for grandparents, bury the dead and hope for something better. Whose children play shoeless in the dirt, proudly go to school, grin and wave at fortunate folks in passing cars, and dream of a life like that. There are millions and millions of these people. They endure economic hardship and still find love, happiness and peace in poverty. We can learn much from them.

We've heard stories of travelers returning to Africa to teach school, open an orphanage or help develop clean water supplies or sanitary living conditions. Bless them; they get it. But does it matter if the needy are in Maputo or Medford?

Africa insistently asks: Are your eyes blind?

Luanda city center

The Four Corners of the World

Friday, March 24th

The Zuiderdam is dead in the water at "Null Island," an imaginary spot in the Atlantic at 0°N-0°-E-0°S-0°W, where the equator meets the prime meridian. We are blocking the intersection. Parked with portside in the Western Hemisphere, the bow in the Northern Hemisphere, starboard in the Eastern Hemisphere and the stern in the Southern Hemisphere. How about that? The Zuiderdam is sitting atop the four corners of the world. Disappointingly, there's no monument sign for photo ops and selfies. And there's nary a nautical souvenir shop in sight. I daresay our 2200 passengers and crew would've stampeded any nautical Nordstrom on this spot for a commemorative "0°N-0°E-0°S-0°W, Been there! Done that!" t-shirt. Someone's missing the boat here. (Sorry.)

Earlier this morning the entertainment director and ship's staff put together a King Neptune Ceremony to celebrate the equatorial crossing. The costumed King and Queen conducted initiation rites for various pollywogs aboard, including rigorous testing for seaworthiness. The pageantry included bowing to the King Fish idol, subjection to poolside slathering with pastel gook and then an unceremonious dunking in the pool. All silly and good fun.

If anyone fantasizes about becoming the entertainment director on a world cruise, forget it. Watching Ian work is exhausting. He works 20-hour days, 7 days a week, for four and a half months straight. No time off. I'd wager he hibernates a month after this cruise.

We have a new captain aboard, Frank van der Hoeven, also from the Netherlands. Captain Friso disembarked in Cape Town, and this is Van der Hoeven's first world voyage. Not exactly a rookie however, he's been with HAL since the early 90s and was promoted to captain over 10 years ago. We'll miss Friso, but it's comforting that a Dutchman is still in the wheelhouse.

Above: Albert Bosomtwi-Sam Fishing Market
Below: Takoradi street market

Colorful Takoradi-Sekondi, Ghana

Monday, March 27th

Takoradi and Sekondi are fraternal twin cities just 11 kilometers apart on the south Atlantic coast of Ghana. The port, major markets and government offices are in Takoradi, while the fish harbor and major commercial enterprises are in Sekondi. Whoever is in charge of road maintenance in both cities must be on permanent vacation. Paved roads are perforated by potholes, saturated by dust and clogged by traffic. I couldn't find a pothole that had been repaired. Apparently, once paved, roads are just allowed to disintegrate. To dust they do return. Inexplicably, the freelance car wash business is booming, with private hand washers at major intersections. With busy roadways blanketed by dust, why bother with a wash? Especially by a guy standing in the mud, holding a dirty towel and a bucket. Clean tires are as rare in Ghana as snowballs.

Ghana is a relatively stable and prosperous African ally of the U.S. But that stability, like Mozambique's, is being threatened by years-long al Qaeda and Islamic State insurgencies along its northern border. Ghana is predominantly Christian in the south and Muslim in the north. Islamist extremists recruit young Muslim militants and instigate conflicts between local ethnic groups and tribal leaders. According to an article appearing in today's Wall Street Journal, "Both Ghanaian and U.S. officials fear that al Qaeda militants...could take advantage of the tensions to establish a beachhead in Ghana." Once established, it would "give al Qaeda access to revenue from trade through Atlantic ports," including Takoradi. While Ghana is relatively prosperous by African standards, it remains poor by world standards, with per capita income at about $5,500 a year, after adjusting for purchasing power parity. Still, life in Ghana is much better than in many of its neighbors. People in these twin cities live in poor housing, but not shanties. Most have fairly reliable electric service, running water and flushing toilets.

The primary employment in Sekondi is fishing, and last Saturday morning the intensely odorous Albert Bosomtwi-Sam Fishing Market was thronged with shoppers. Most arrived on foot wearing flip flops, sandals or crocs. The fishermen are privateers who use large wooden vessels called "canoes." Before heading to sea, they buy ice blocks from the harbor ice plant to preserve the daily catch. Upon return, the catch is turned over to female brokers who negotiate prices. We're told the fishermen use female brokers because they are "tougher negotiators," and "men are too soft."

At the bustling market, varieties of fresh caught fish were displayed on ice in plastic bags, buckets, aluminum tubs, or laid out on tabletops. Some vendors were shaded under tarps, others worked under the baking sun. Also lining the sunny docks were tubs of live seafood, including crab, lobster and slimy sea snails as big as your head. Multiple vendors offered colorful fresh fruits and veggies. Women with aluminum tubs on their heads, weaved in and around the crowds, hawking fresh and dried fish, soft drinks, snacks and plastic footwear.

The men don't negotiate and don't carry tubs on their heads. Men fish. I asked for the predominant species harvested off the coast of Sekondi. Our guide replied, "Fish." In addition to packing the fresh catch on ice, other sanitary standards are enforced at the harbor market. A sign in front of the tiny Canoe Owners Association office read "DON'T URINATE HERE," with a Pictionary rendering of a guy taking a whiz within a red, diagonally crossed circle. Is anywhere else ok?

In downtown Takoradi, the once thriving Takoradi Market Circle is gone. The enormous 90 year old circular market was shut down in 2021 due to overcrowding, unsanitary conditions and fire hazard. In its place a new center is under construction that will house over 2400 stores and 33 restaurants, plus parking spaces, union offices, a police station, fire station, post office, medical clinic and administration offices. It's hard to imagine all that on the circular site of the old market.

All 2400 stores (surely vendor stalls) expected inside the new market appear to have temporary quarters on the perimeter of the old circle. And I'm guessing most of the million-plus Takoradi Sekondi residents were shopping today. It looked like mardi-gras, and it took our driver an hour to creepy-crawl through the throngs milling about the vendor booths. Our minibus idled around the circle until someone spotted a mango vendor and asked the driver to stop. There was no place to pull over, so he just stopped in the crowd. We hopped out, and wouldn't you know it? Next to the mangos was an African "Fabrics-R-Us" under a tarp. Christeen and friends plunged into a kaleidoscopic fabric heaven. The fabrics were fabulous, reflecting the brilliantly colorful and creatively designed print dresses and scarves worn by Ghanaian women. Christeen wanted to buy, buy, buy. Thankfully, she is limited to two suitcases and a carryon, all of which are full.

I took dozens of photos. Ghana was special today, not only for the beautiful people, brilliant blue skies and deep violet shadows, but also the special character of cluttered sidewalks, tatty motorbikes, faded signs and shuttered storefronts. Everything seemed picture perfect. Without exception, the Ghanaians we met were kind, friendly and welcoming. We had been repeatedly advised against taking photos of policemen, yet one of our group asked a policeman if he'd mind a photo with her friend. He nodded politely and she snapped away.

Hard to comprehend, amongst such friendliness, beauty and peace, that just a few hundred kilometers north, militant extremists are working to destroy it all.

Abidjan Boys Orphanage at Bingerville

Tuesday, March 28th

     The Abidjan Boys Orphanage is located in a suburb called Bingerville, which was the capital of the Ivory Coast from 1909 to 1934. In 1912 a three-story, New Orleans-style governor's palace was built in Bingerville. It took 7 years to build the palatial palace with a majestic double staircase entry and signature louvered window shutters, a la the French Quarter. Various colonial administrators resided in the palace, known as "the house of 100 doors," until 1934, when the capital was moved to Abidjan. In 1935, the palace was converted to a boarding house for mixed-race orphans. The orphans were born of French colonist dalliances with native women, in many instances, "colonial rape." According to a "Petit Fute" opinion on Google search, the orphanage was originally "meant to welcome the little bastards of the colony." Later the orphanage took in war orphans of fallen French soldiers, in recognition of the "sacrifice of their fathers." Over the years, orphans were placed by the Red Cross and others. Then in 1972, the girls were moved to a girls-only facility, and Bingerville was dedicated to boys.

     Today the palace is stubbornly weathered from decades of deferred maintenance and dilapidation. The orphanage is surrounded by a formidable block wall with a locked iron entry gate. The circular driveway contains broken pavement and deep potholes. Sun-bleached decaying buildings dot the grassy grounds, including multiple dormitories, classrooms, a mess hall and a laundry. Additionally, there's a picnic canopy and a relatively new (and padlocked?) outdoor sports court. A sign above the court proclaims, "Bingerville Dreams Big."

Clotheslines outside the dormitories are loaded with colorful wash flapping silently in the sunny breeze. Inside the dormitories, bunk beds line the walls with bare mattresses, no linens and no pictures above the beds. Behind one of the classrooms, a faded broken bus, on the side "Boys Orphanage at Bingerville" painted in French, settles in the red clay.

Under the picnic canopy we were welcomed by the African administrator, who described current operations in French, while our guide interpreted. The orphanage capacity is 250; currently there are 188 boys in residence, ages 5 to 23. The school campus includes offices and classrooms for elementary through high school. Each boy is required to attend school on site and is responsible for his own laundry and sleeping area, together with various assigned chores. The administrator said most of the boys were "motherless and fatherless," meaning either both parents were deceased or both had abandoned the child. In certain cases, a boy is admitted where a living parent is incapable of providing for him. However, no child can be admitted with a capable living parent. The orphanage is funded primarily by the government, with supplemental private donations. As the administrator spoke, about 30 slender young boys sat on the side attentively checking us out. Following his remarks, a boy turned on a boombox and they performed an impromptu freestyle dance to French rock n' roll. They laughed and giggled and entirely enjoyed themselves. We gave them a standing ovation.

While searching my tiny stateroom closet the other day, I experienced clothing loathing. I had packed too many clothes, so I filled a bag for the orphanage. After repeated calls to guest services, I was told donations were not allowed due to "import restrictions." Others on our excursion tried to make similar donations of school supplies and were rejected as well. However, before we departed the orphanage, HAL donated a portion of our excursion fees, to which several of us added cash.

As we prepared to board the bus, I bumped fists with the boys, took some photos and said, "*Au revoir.*" Looking into those eager faces, I wondered about the back stories. Sadly, my French is limited to *bonjour, au revoir*, and *merci beaucoup.* Despite dilapidated facilities and apparent funding challenges, the boys at Bingerville are far better off than they would be on the streets of Abidjan.

I've thought about mailing direct donations to Bingerville. The funding needs are apparent and dramatic. For unknown reasons we were not invited inside the majestic old governor's palace. That was strange, but what gave me pause was parked under the shade of a magnolia tree behind the building: a shiny new black Mercedes sedan.

Will donations mailed actually benefit the boys? There must be a way.

Boys at Bingerville

Banjul, The Republic of The Gambia

Wednesday, March 29th

The Republic of The Gambia is tiny, at less than 30 miles wide it's the smallest country in continental Africa. It's bisected by the Gambia River and bordered on three sides by Senegal, with the Atlantic Ocean bordering the west. Gambia's population is over 2.4 million, with nearly 500,000 in the area of Banjul, the capital city. About half the people live in poverty, with a per capita annual GDP of about $2100. Gambia is 96% Muslim and, while English is the official language, it's considered the first language of only a small portion of the population, since there are numerous indigenous dialects.

Banjul is located on an island where the Gambia River flows into the Atlantic. Yesterday morning, while riding the shuttle to the historic Albert Market, we were struck by pervasive urban poverty. We saw no KFCs or McDonalds or any global franchise stores, only shabbiness and decay with older vehicles, wheelbarrows, carts, bicycles and people clogging the narrow streets. I thought our driver made a wrong turn as we followed a winding dirt alley past rotting trash and thoroughly scavenged junk piles. Presently, he stopped and opened the bus door. There was no "Albert Market" sign, no stores, no parking lot and no street signs. Just a narrow dirt path into a labyrinthine maze of crowded shanty stalls. We had arrived at a massive flea market. No one on the shuttle moved and someone mumbled, "Are we supposed to get out?" Another said, "Where's the next stop?" I got off and asked the driver if there was another stop. He shook his head, "Only stop." A few trickled off the bus, but most stared through the windows mumbling to themselves "You gotta be kidding," and returned to the ship. As the shuttle drove away, I wondered what we were getting into.

We were informed that Albert Market was founded in the mid-1800s by British traders. Today, it retains all the creature comforts of an 1850s flea market, except that it's certainly far more crowded. As we entered the narrow, winding dirt pathway that led through the market, we stuck out like pallbearers in pink pajamas. The local artisans and vendors were peddling clothing, fabrics, sandals, baskets, native jewelry, wood carvings, used electronics, canned goods and of course, fresh fish, meats, fruits and vegetables. We made an unfortunate turn directly into the fresh meat section. Pungent fish odor instantly knickered the nostrils and penetrated our skin, hair and clothing. (Last night on my pillow I could still smell it.) Fresh fish and crustaceans were laid (without ice) on tables, boxes and on the ground. Flies swarmed all over the seafood, meats, fruits and vegetables. Dogs, cats and kittens casually did their business in the dirt and roamed free. We were told the locals shop for groceries at Albert Market. It looked plenty scary to me, but it had to be less expensive than a local supermarket. The Gambians must have kamikaze digestive and immune systems.

We wound our way beyond the decaying fish, past dozens of clothing, fabric, leather, arts and jewelry stalls. The colorful fabrics and designs were sensational. In several stalls, tailors sewed dresses, shirts and trousers on site. Doesn't fit? The seamstress will alter it on the spot. We found making eye contact meant, "I wanna buy something." The merchant would instantly pounce. Walking away without making a purchase was nearly impossible. Turn away, and the seller would place a bracelet on your arm and say, "My gift to you, my friend." I refused all gifts but bought several bracelets. Christeen quickly became frustrated, since she likes shopping more than buying. During the course of a few purchases, the process became exhausting. We finally surrendered and returned to the ship.

At the dock, Christeen was delighted to find a line of eager Gambian merchants waiting to pounce.

Albert Market tailor and seamstress

Dakar Delete; Violent Protests in Senegal

Thursday, March 30th

The Dakar pilot boarded in the dark early this morning and deftly maneuvered the Zuiderdam to the dock. Fierce fish odor permeated the air as Dakar port hands secured the ship. We proceeded to deck three, awaiting disembarkation clearance. After about thirty minutes Captain Van der Hoeven announced that "due to civil unrest, protests and violence," all excursions were canceled and no passengers would be allowed to disembark. He added however, that the Zuiderdam would spend the day at port, pending the loading of eight shipping containers of fresh meat, produce and hotel supplies.

The dock remained quiet all morning. Later, we were informed that, due to political unrest, the containers were not "cleared" and couldn't be loaded. HAL scrambled, but couldn't find, other local suppliers. We waited all day and finally departed for the Canary Islands with no restock.

Very strange stuff. Seems they could've loaded the supplies, but who knows? There may have been some fear of sabotage. We're disappointed we couldn't disembark, but a tour bus would be easy prey for thugs seeking notoriety or ransom or political clout. As recently as last week, local news reported, "Demonstrators in Dakar burned tires and set fire to buses and a large supermarket." The Senegal demonstrators supported an opposition leader who'd been arrested by the ruling party. Police dispersed crowds with tear gas. Probably a wise decision to stay aboard.

Returning to our staterooms after dinner, we received a note from Henk, the hotel general manager. He assured us he was working to get us re-supplied in Tenerife, but in the meantime, "There is plenty of wine and toilet paper aboard." Henk covers the essentials.

Looks like Spam steaks for dinner tomorrow and nix the side salad.

Two Terrific Canaries

Sunday, April 2nd

The Canary Islands are an autonomous community of Spain, in the Atlantic about 60 miles west of Morocco. The islands comprise an archipelago of seven main islands and dozens of smaller ones, with a combined population of over 2.2 million, most Spanish Catholics. After a month of sailing around southern and western Africa, we were delighted to be back on the "islands." Both Santa Cruz, Tenerife and Arrecife, Lanzarote have alluring white sand beaches, intriguing histories, slumbering volcanos, temperate weather and pristine Atlantic seascapes.

The islands are not named after a bird. "Canary" is believed to be derived from the Latin word for dog, canaria. One theory is that Spanish explorers, confronted by vast quantities of resident large dogs, named the islands Canariae Insulae or "islands of the dogs." But it's only a theory, as the origin of the dog population is a matter of conjecture. Some have blamed the Romans, but can't explain why they would bring big dogs. The canary bird species is actually native to the islands and is named after the islands.

In Santa Cruz, our bus followed serpentine switchbacks to the top of the Anaga Mountains. I've seen some sensational motorcycle roads, and TF-12 over Anaga certainly qualifies, except for tortoising tour buses. The buses block both lanes of the narrow road while negotiating the switchbacks. On a fast bike, a blocked switchback could be deadly. Notwithstanding, we saw multiple bullet bikers on the road. They must be expert bus detectors.

The Canary Islands are a prime vacation destination for winter-weary Europeans. The climate is sunny and warm and the beaches, cafes, shops and resorts are relaxing and reasonably priced. Our native narrator put it this way: "North Americans have Hawaii, yes? Europeans have Canary Islands!"

We didn't see many big dogs, but we saw plenty of chihuahuas. Must be the Spanish influence. In Arrecife, we had a lovely walkabout and toured the historic church of San Gines, built in 1574 and entirely rebuilt in 1667, after a flood. Saint Gines is Arrecife's patron saint. The building is a church not a cathedral, and is accordingly rather pedestrian by Catholic standards.

Christeen especially loved the Canaries for two reasons: a double strawberry and pistachio gelato in a wafer cone, and the four liter and a half bottles of Pcpsi she smuggled on the Zuiderdam. She has large pockets.

Christeen and Pepsi

Happy Agadir, Morocco

Tuesday, April 4th

Windy and cool today in Agadir, Morocco. We're sailing north beyond the equator and the weather is already changing. Time to stow the island wear. This morning we took a 4x4 "adventure" from Agadir to rural Paradise Valley. Our Moroccan driver spoke fluent "good morning." Beyond that, he remained mute except for occasional Arabic outbursts at errant drivers, bikers, hikers and goats. Disappointingly, he didn't venture off road and never put the Toyota 4x4 in four-wheel drive. The passing landscape looked similar to east San Diego county, between Julian and Borrego: dry, dusty sunbaked hills with wild olive trees and mesquite-like scrub. Plus, random sheep and goat herds.

We stopped at a women's co-op called Moroccan Magic Products. The path behind the modest roadside storefront led through a small botanical garden to an open shed shading several round tables. Along the path, two women in traditional hijabs and brightly colored robes were seated on mosaic tiles, backs against a wall, crushing nuts using small rocks on large stones. We were invited to sit at the tables, and a young woman in a magenta hijab, loose floral print top and thongs offered us flat bread with locally processed honey, peanut butter, olive oil, almond butter and argan oil. She said that until last month, it hadn't rained in Paradise Valley in four years. Seemed an odd spot for a botanical garden. Obviously there's a good water well.

After a short garden show-and-tell, our hostess led us back to the female nutcrackers and explained that they were harvesting argan nuts. Argan trees grow only in southwest Morocco, and oil from the nut is believed to boost the immune system, lower bad cholesterol, stimulate hair growth, eliminate wrinkles and cure eczema. All timely geezer therapeutics. Because processing is labor intensive and oil yields are tiny, the finished products cost a fortune. Notwithstanding, we bought eczema cream, hair oil, skin oil and lotion. Don't ask.

We made another stop at a roadside souvenir store with two signs painted in big block letters across the top: One read "W C" and the other read "Toilet." Clearly the highest and best use of that roadside amenity. Inside, the owner, in a dusty faded robe, spoke sufficient English. To him, "no" meant "absolutely, gotta have it." I made the mistake of letting him see me pick up a crystallized rock. He promptly approached, certified its rarity and distinction and named a price. I put the rock down and said, "No, thanks," He cut the price by a third and stuck the rock in a bag. I said, "No thanks" again and walked out. He followed me out and dropped his price again. I got in the Toyota, and he handed the bag through the window and said, "Ok, what you pay?"

Morocco has a population of over 37 million and virtually all are Muslim. From Paradise Valley, we drove through villages where most women wore the traditional hijab and many men wore an ankle-length long sleeved "thobe" similar to a tunic. In coastal Agadir, dress varied from traditional to westernized. Along the beachfront, most dressed like Europeans. In fact, one beachfront billboard pictured women in bikinis. Agadir was almost entirely destroyed by a massive earthquake in 1960. It has since been rebuilt and is considered the most modern city in Morocco. We took an evening stroll on the windy beachfront promenade. Someone said Agadir is intent on becoming the Miami Beach of north Africa. It looks like it. The beaches are wide and spotless, and the promenade is lined with inviting shops, restaurants and nightclubs.

In Morocco, the observance of Ramadan by Muslims began on

March 22 and will end on April 21st. During Ramadan, fasting from dawn until sunset is required for all adults.. Consequently, when we arrived at the beach around 5:30 pm, none of the restaurants, including an oceanfront McDonalds, were open. By the time we left, the restaurants had opened, and families were arriving at the beach with animated kids and loaded picnic baskets to celebrate breaking the fast.

All were smiling, hungry and happy.

Roadside souvenir shop

"Don't You Know We're Riding on the Marrakech Express?"

Friday, April 7th

Yesterday a 12-hour bus excursion took us from Casablanca, Morocco, to Marrakech, the oldest (circa 1070) imperial city in the kingdom. In my head, Crosby Stills and Nash performed "Marrakech Express" all along the highway. Marrakech is a big city, with metro population over a million; but we spent our time within the walls of the ancient fortified city, now the teeming Souks (Arabic for market) of Marrakech.

Our Moroccan guide apologized for his heavily accented English, but observed that his English was probably better than our Arabic. Regarding Ramadan, he confessed, "I'm fasting today, not by conviction, but by habit." He added, "I have great respect for all believers in all faiths." Out the window, the dusty haze above the rolling landscape southeast of Casablanca looked like California's eastern Coachella Valley, dotted with sheep. A shepherd wearing a dark full length thobe and carrying a staff tended each flock. The movie *Casablanca,* in which Humphrey Bogart charmed Ingrid Bergman away from her husband, was not filmed at Rick's Café in Casablanca but rather at a mock-up of the same in Hollywood. Happily, we skipped Rick's Cafe.

Along the way, our guide explained the five "pillars" of Islam: 1) Faith (there is no god but God), 2) Prayer (five times a day], 3) Almsgiving to the poor, 4) Fasting (for 30 days during Ramadan), and 5) Pilgrimage to Mecca. These five are considered requisite for Muslims to inherit the kingdom of God.

"What happens if you don't get to Mecca?" I asked.

He smiled and said, "Do you want my answer or the official answer? The official answer is you must do it in your lifetime if you can afford it. It's expensive, as Mecca is in faraway Saudi Arabia. However, if you work, save for it, and still can't afford it, then you get a pass." After a pause, he continued, "Do you want to know what I think? I don't give a damn about it."

Islam has two official holidays on the lunar or Islamic calendar: the last day of Ramadan, Eid al-Fitr, or Festival of the Sweets, and then 2 months and 10 days after the end of Ramadan, Eid al-Adha, or Feast of Sacrifice. The guide explained that the sheep tended by lone shepherds along the highway were being fattened for the Feast of Sacrifice. The feast honors Abraham's willingness to sacrifice Isaac, and the sacrificial lamb. In commemoration, Muslim families sacrifice and then consume a lamb. Whatever is left over is given to the poor. Buying a lamb before Eid al-Adha seems akin to buying a turkey before Thanksgiving, except that sheep are bought on the hoof. In large cities like Casablanca, the buying and selling of live animals is hectic just before feast day. The animal is consumed, but the valuable hides, wool, hoofs and horns are to be discarded. Our guide considered the discarding an absurd waste in a country where so many are so poor.

The souks market was packed with merchant stalls, eateries, noxious annoying motorbikes, dilapidated donkey carts, beggars, meddlesome monkeys, snake charmers and hordes of shoppers and hawkers. After a couple of hours winding through the kaleidoscopic maze, constantly evading mayhem or death by manic mopeds or dilatory donkeys, we visited the ruins of the circa 1590 El Badi Palace and the lavish circa 1860 Bahia Palace. We were led by a Marrakech guide, but the souks were so crowded we were unable to stop and shop for fear of losing our way. We finally entered a side alley and turned into a dark, tiled hallway that led to an ornate, windowless, high-ceilinged dining room with massive pillars and mosaic tiled walls. Multiple crystal chandeliers hung from the tiled ceiling. A couple dozen dining tables surrounded a hexagonal stand at the center of the room. Loud Moroccan music played on an amplified five string oud, accompanied by a single-headed drum called a darbouka, obliterated any table conversation. Lunch consisted of flatbread with various spice dips, plus roast chicken, rice, olives, carrots and squash. As soon as lunch arrived, a bejeweled Shikhat belly dancer took the center stand, covered head-to-toe in a shimmering gown revealing only her eyes. A golden candelabra featuring 8 lighted candles crowned her head. She wiggled her ample belly and bottom, twirling to the snappy tempo of the screeching Moroccan music until her candles finally flamed out. Then she stepped off the stand and danced from table to table. American dollars soon lined her waistband. The entire noisy routine was long and wearying. It finally ended in glorious silence. Within minutes, however, another slit-eyed belly dancer took center stage and tortured us all over again.

We exited the restaurant to the market square which looked remarkably similar to the spot where Indiana Jones pulled a pistol and shot the black-robed saber-wielding bad guy in *Raiders of the Lost Ark.* (That was filmed in Cairo). Snake charmers, chattering monkeys, trinket hawkers and fruit vendors littered the square. It was a place we didn't want to leave, but by late afternoon, the tour guide was calling. Before boarding the bus, we walked around the 12th century Koutoubia Mosque and its towering minaret but were unable to enter because of Ramadan.

Magical Marrakech. What a place.

Most slept as dusk settled over the hills on the long ride back to Casablanca. I wanted to see if any of the shepherds were still "watching their flocks by night." Remarkably, some were.

It made me wonder, what could be more difficult than standing in the sun all day in a treeless open field, clad head to toe in a dark gown, watching sheep graze?

Marrakech belly dancer

Malaga, Spain: Historic, Artsy and Majestic

Saturday, April 8th

The Strait of Gibraltar, separating Morocco from Spain at the southern tip of the Iberian Peninsula, is a scant 8 miles wide. But even that close, Malaga, Spain is a world apart from Tangier, Morocco. We arrived in Malaga on this brilliantly sunny Saturday morning, the day before Easter. Spain is almost evenly divided between believers and non-believers, with believers being overwhelmingly Roman Catholic. Procession routes for yesterday's Good Friday celebrations were marked by grandstands, shade tarps and folding chairs that will be used again for the Easter celebrations tomorrow. Malaga is a glorious historic city on the Mediterranean seacoast dating back to about 770 BC. Multiple cruise ships are docked in the harbor, and today this blooming city was bustling with tourists from Europe and around the world.

We waited in line at the celebrated Cathedral of Malaga, built between 1528 and 1782. I wrote a few weeks ago about the fabulous Sydney Cathedral. Well, Malaga Cathedral is unbelievably fabulous-er. Everything is overwhelming: massive Renaissance architecture, centuries-worn stone flooring, Romanesque interior columns and porticos, soaring clerestory ceilings, banks of brass organ pipes, exquisite marble and bronze sculptures, ornate woodwork, priceless oil paintings, resplendent stained glass, glorious candelabras and altars and an interior slathered in brilliant gold leaf. Could any tribute to God be too majestic? How the Church in the 16th, 17th and 18th-centuries constructed such an extravagant edifice is unimaginable. On the other hand, I wonder if God was embarrassed by all this grandeur while Andalusian peasants suffered in poverty and privation.

Pablo Picasso was born October 25, 1881, in Malaga, and there is a superb Picasso Museum in town. Picasso was a gifted artist as his early representational work demonstrates. I've never thought much of his later work, but what do I know? During his lifetime, Picasso became wealthy and famous with legions of admirers and collectors. His major works today bring stratospheric prices at auction. We attend art museums because original art is always far more brilliant and expressive than photographic images. Today, I found an exception. While I was delighted to visit the Picasso Museum, I wasn't impressed by his later original works. Many looked like sloppy, unfinished afterthoughts. But again, what do I know?

After the Picasso Museum, we walked to the Carmen Thyssen Museum, located in a restored 16th century city palace. Baroness Carmen Thyssen is a Spanish socialite and art collector and a former Miss Spain (1961), whose third marriage to billionaire Baron Hans Heinrich Thyssen no doubt helps fund her art proclivities. She opened the Malaga Museum in 2011, and it's a gem. One of few "new" art museums that is not entirely, or even partially, devoted to contemporary art. Over the years, she collected some old masters, but the Thyssen Collection emphasizes evocative 19th and early 20th-century Spanish artists. On this very busy Easter weekend, we waited over half an hour in line to enter the Picasso Museum and then struggled to get near the paintings amidst the thronging crowds. But there were no lines in the Carmen Thyssen Museum, and we casually strolled through expansive exhibit halls with a handful of other patrons. A far superior experience than the Picasso Museum, IMHO.

Especial Easter en Cadiz, España

Easter Sunday, April 9th

The historic "circled by the sea" Old Town Cadiz lies immediately opposite the cruise ship dock. The signature structure within Old Town is the Cadiz Cathedral, constructed beginning in 1722 and completed a mere *116 years* later in 1838. Not only did multiple generations of craftsmen work on the project, but also successive generations of architects and designers. Consequently, what was originally designed in the baroque style evolved through rococo and gothic elements and was completed in the neoclassical style. Notwithstanding design evolution, the final product is massive, solid, stately and elegant. Not as fabulous as Malaga Cathedral, but plenty impressive.

On this gloriously sunny Easter morning, we arrived at the Cadiz Cathedral just as Easter Mass was celebrated. We joined thousands of the faithful outside the cathedral as a resplendent Easter Processional exited the massive wooden doors. Dozens of saints lead the procession carrying staffs topped with ornate gold or silver crucifixes. From the rear cathedral doors, a glittering golden ceremonial barge, crowned with a life-sized statue of the resurrected Savior was carried aloft, followed by a uniformed brass band and drum corps. The shrill brass and percussion music proclaimed, "He is Risen!" The entire procession led through the narrow streets of Old Town toward another cathedral a few blocks away. It was a masterful demonstration of devotion; the Catholics are pomp and ceremony virtuosos.

In the afternoon, we toured the imposing cathedral and underground burial crypt. The original architects understood underground construction. The impressive and expansive 300-year-old crypt is original, and is as dry and sound as if completed last year. (Of course, electricity has been added, along with the remains of several more recent deceased saints.) Once outside, I climbed the winding stone ramp up the 130 foot Levante Bell Tower. Through an open alcove I took some spectacular Cadiz skyline and bayfront photos. I had noted, but paid little attention to, a small sign posting the chiming of the bells. At 3:00 pm, I was pulverized by the deafening ringing of a massive brass bell directly over my head.

Happy Easter Sunday. I've had my bell rung.

Levante Tower bell

Perfectly Portugal

Tuesday, April 11th

Portugal, a narrow rectangle bounded on opposite sides by Spain and the Atlantic Ocean, is endowed with mild weather, romantic beauty, an endless coastline and fascinating history. During the 15th and 16th-centuries, this tiny country (about the size of Indiana) became one of the world's great empires. Its influence throughout the world is astounding. Today over 265 million people worldwide speak Portuguese, yet the country itself has a population of less than 11 million.

Nearly 30 years ago, Christeen and I flew to Lisbon, and stayed in the beautiful and quaint municipality of Murtosa at the family home of our friends John and Rose Martins. During our week-long stay, we were served by John's elderly aunt, a nun in a nearby convent. She scheduled her convent vacation time in order to cook, clean and do laundry for us. Undoubtedly, she has by now found her place amongst the angelic hosts of heaven.

Lisbon has changed much in the past 30 years, but it's still as charming as I remember. Our early morning cruise up the river Tagus, from its estuary at the Atlantic to the port at Lisbon, took two hours. All along the riverbank, ancient castles and fortifications tantalize history buffs with visions of successive Celt, Phoenician, Roman, Barbarian and Muslim conquerors and occupiers. In 1147, Alfonso I of Portugal reconquered Lisbon, re-established Christianity and drove the Muslims and their Arabic dialect out of the country. Following the re-conquest, all Islamic mosques were either destroyed or converted to churches. In the

16th and 17th-centuries, Portugal became the world naval power and Lisbon, the European trading center for spices, slaves, sugar and textiles. Unfortunately, on November 1, 1755 an earthquake destroyed an estimated 85% of Lisbon and killed about 20% of the population. Accordingly, much of Lisbon today dates from the late 18th century or reflects reconstruction of centuries old earthquake ruins.

We took an afternoon excursion to Obidos, a medieval walled city about 100 kilometers north of Lisbon. The Obidos region was historically occupied by Celts, Phoenicians, Romans and Moors (Muslims). Around 713, the Moors built a castle and walled fortification around Obidos, which stands today, despite damage during the 1755 earthquake. The narrow, terraced, winding and colorful streets reminded us of the markets at Marrakech, thronged with tourists and shoppers. We visited the ancient Church of Santa Maria (circa 1148, reconstructed in 1571), the site of the August 15, 1441 wedding of King Alfonso V to his cousin, Princess Isabella of Coimbra, when they were respectively, 10 and 8 years old. Sadly, Queen Isabella lived only until age 23; her death possibly the result of strategic poisoning.

Today the sacred edifice of Santa Maria, with its adjacent cobblestone courtyard, remains a popular wedding venue. It's easy to understand that, but thankfully, the traditional age for marriage among eager nuptial newbies has risen significantly.

As we pondered the receding Lisbon skyline, we repeatedly heard the comment, "What's not to like?" I didn't find much; even the city's graffiti was unusually artful. Indeed Portugal, because of its great climate, quality of life and reasonable cost of living, is an oft-cited retirement destination.

It could be close to as good as it gets.

A Crowned A Coruna and Bye Bye Brest

Wednesday, April 12th

Last night clairvoyant Christeen finally unpacked her woolens, down vest and parka, then packed away her swimsuit, shorts and short sleeved tops. This morning just before sunrise, cold slashing rain pelted the Zuiderdam as we cruised the north shore of Spain into A Coruna. By 8:45, the steady rain slowed to spanking spittle. Moments later, howling winds aloft shoved the snarky storm clouds to the sea and carried a cumulus crown atop sunny, windy A Coruna.

At 9:00, Captain Van der Hoeven announced those pesky winds were part of a low pressure system creating havoc in the Bay of Biscay, off the coast of France. Enough to delay our sail away from A Coruna by 6 hours and to delete Brest, France, from tomorrow's itinerary. The revised plan is to stay out of the Bay of Biscay and steam directly to Weymouth (Portland), England, arriving half-day early. Even skipping the worst of the storm, we are expected to encounter 40-knot headwinds and 20-foot swells tomorrow. Bummed about missing Brest, but I'm looking forward to cruising on this 82,000 ton boogie board in the morning.

We were accosted at the dock by the usual flotilla of local tour operators and taxi drivers. We waved them off, walked around the windy boat harbor and then, with friends Ron and Valentina, took a bus tour of city sights. We stopped at Jardin de San Carlos, a small botanical flower garden in Old Town. Few flowers were blooming or even budding here in early April, but we leisurely walked the muddy cobblestones amid rain splattered greenery. Oddly, Ron and Valentina did not return to the bus at the appointed time. Our young tour guide searched and fretted for 15 minutes. Finally, after others demanded, "leave them," she assured us this rarely happens and we drove on. Ron and Valentina had never missed a bus, but what to do? The botanical garden was within walking distance to the port, so we weren't overly concerned, but it was plenty weird.

We finished the tour just in time for the shopkeeper's siesta in the city center. Customarily in Spain, most shops close from 2:00 to 4:00 pm, or whenever the napping shopkeeper awakens. We walked in blustery sunshine and shade around the historic municipal plaza and through winding streets of Old Town, past the shuttered storefronts. Happily, we stumbled upon Confiteria La Coruna, an open pastry and sandwich shop. After perfecto ham and cheese croissants, delicately delicious creme pastries and refreshing Coke and Coke Zero, we didn't care whether the shops were open or not.

As it turned out, Ron had breakfasted on pickled herring and raw onion. He explained he forgot his stomach does not tolerate raw onions since gallbladder surgery years ago. By the time our bus stopped at Jardin de San Carlos, Ron's stomach was bloating, and they made a beeline for the ship with Ron passing gas like a methane freighter.

I couldn't understand why anyone would eat a barf bag breakfast. How about pickled oatmeal and raw raisins tomorrow?

Fed Up with France

Friday, April 14th

Walking the surfing Zuiderdam yesterday was somewhat treacherous. Bless-ed handy handrails kept me vertical in the stateroom corridors, but diners and waiters froze as I did the waltzing Matilda to our table. Fortunately, no mashed potato face plants. Conditions have deteriorated this morning with 55-knot winds, outside temps in the low 40s, heavy rolling seas, and pestering rain. Perfect Pendleton weather. We're scheduled for an early arrival in Portland (Weymouth), England around 1:00 pm, but a container ship is rudely docked at our spot.

Captain Van der Hoeven just announced that the national labor strike in France now includes dock workers. Last time we were in France, we accompanied our daughter Mindi to a "study abroad" in Paris. We spent a couple of days in London, got fleeced by a phony ticket seller in the theatre district, then escaped to Paris via bullet train under the English Channel. We were thrilled to visit gay Pariee with the iconic Louvre and D'Orsay Museums. We settled in a charmingly quaint room near both museums and enjoyed a lovely dinner, despite uppity French waiters. Refreshed by morning, we arrived at the Louvre early, only to be greeted by "En Greve!" (On Strike!) signs plastered on the doors. During our 4 days in Paris, both museums remained closed.

Last November I reserved the HAL all day excursion from Le Havre, France to scenic Giverny and Monet's Garden. To prepare, I read another biography of Claude Monet and the Impressionists. That excursion was to be a highlight of this trip. I should've known better. In an effort to save the generous French pension system from bankruptcy, President Macron recently added 2 years to the minimum retirement age. The disgruntled labor unions have the populace in an uproar over it. Frenchies are not having enough babies, hence there are not enough workers to fund massive pensions for swelling numbers of retirees. If they don't extend the retirement age, the pension system (and government) will ultimately collapse, and then no one gets a pension. Unionistas could care less. Socialists believe the government can tax the wealthy and print money ad infinitum. That works until all the wealthy are broke, or have fled to the Cayman Islands, and hyperinflation from massive money printing has destroyed the economy.

With no dock workers, Captain Van der Hoveven had no choice but to scratch France. The good news is, the day after tomorrow we will add Dover, England to the itinerary in lieu of Le Havre. Who knows, there may be a painting in those scenic white cliffs of Dover.

Postscript: It's now 8:00 pm local time. We remain patiently anchored off the coast of Portland, England. Turns out bad weather also delayed the container ship handling. To minimize unacceptable rolling and pitching, the Zuiderdam thrusters will be deployed throughout the night to keep the bow into the wind. Hopefully we'll weigh anchor before dawn and enjoy a wet April day docked in jolly Portland.

Love those Brits

I just realized it's Tax Day in the USA. Oblivion is one of the many benefits of floating the world. Yesterday I wrote about being fleeced in London. There are bad people everywhere and whoever did that is not typical of the British we've met. They are delightful people, and we love visiting Britain. The Brits have boundless humor, a fascinating history, delightful food, charming countrysides, rugged coastlines, sexy sports cars, crazy motorbikes and lousy weather. They also drive on the wrong side of the road.

In Portland we were greeted by a host of happy Brit ambassadors and given free street maps and a shuttle ride to Weymouth. On our walk from the shuttle stop to the harbor, we encountered a group of swimmers in the windy bay. The outside temperature was below 50 degrees, and the water had to be colder. The swimmers were wearing only swimsuits and goosebumps. I asked two young women who were about to take the plunge if they were certified insane. "On the contrary," they replied, "before our daily cold water swim, we were emotional, pill-popping wrecks. Now we take no medications whatsoever!" Humm. Just wait until their brains thaw.

The day turned clear and crisp, and by midday locals in t-shirts and shorts crowded the windy beach along the harbor. We zipped our hoodies against the wind and wondered if we were nuts or they were nuts. We stopped for lunch at The Boat Takeaway, a waterfront wooden quonset hut. We ordered fish and chips, thinking we'd get some undersized, overpriced amusement park food on a paper plate. Wrong. The portions were huge, the golden fish was mild and delicately battered, and the chips were big and crispy. With a side salad and extra tartar sauce, it made for a delicious monster lunch.

We spent the afternoon in the circa 1860 Nothe Fort in Weymouth and the circa 1540 Portland Castle. By late afternoon the wind had blown itself out and sharp shadows defined the ancient castle. English history is captivating, and the staff at both Nothe Fort and Portland Castle were helpful, friendly and gregarious. They gave life to these great places.

Back on ship, about 50 members of a community choir from Weymouth assembled on the dock and serenaded us for the better part of an hour. Following each song, we clapped and waved, and they clapped and waved back. It was like we were a family embarking on a distant voyage. Then volunteers from Nothe Fort, including four period-uniformed officers, placed a 19th-century cannon on the dock. They loaded the cannon and waited until the securing ropes were drawn back to the ship. Then they fired, reloaded and fired twice more. Each massive blast rattled the Zuiderdam.

A cheery sail away salute. Gotta love those Brits.

The Boat Takeaway

Strategic Dover Castle

Sunday, April 16th

Dover Castle is a historic above-and-below-ground military defense complex atop the white cliffs of Dover. The site is crowned by a circa 1180 King Henry II castle, on the highest rampart. The castle is surrounded by an impassable deep moat, with entry points accessible solely by drawbridge. Some Dover structures date to the 2nd-century, with many from the 12th or 13th-centuries.

The castle was continually garrisoned into the 20th century, and during World War II, Dover became the headquarters for the British Admiralty's regional command. That regional command was secreted in 3.8 *miles* of underground tunnels carved under the castle out of the stable, but relatively easy to excavate, white chalk of Dover (hence the "white cliffs"). Vice Admiral Bertram Ramsey conducted covert strategic naval and air operations from the secret tunnels. Including the famous Operation Dunkirk where some 338,000 defeated allied soldiers were evacuated across the English Channel from France. The Germans had crushed the retreating allies at Dunkirk beach during the Battle of France, but inexplicably the Nazis didn't finish them off. At the time, Winston Churchill called the allied defeat a "colossal military disaster." German General von Rundstedt, with Hitler's approval, halted his armies and turned final Allied army destruction over the German Luftwaffe bombers. The Allied forces were sitting ducks, but the German army didn't advance. Then during the week of evacuation, God provided dense low-lying cloud cover over the channel and Vice Admiral Ramsey sent every naval and private vessel available to the rescue. Luftwaffe bombing through the clouds had limited effect, and the rescue became a turning point in the war, allowing Churchill to regroup and fight another day. Castle staff told us Hitler never authorized the bombing of Dover. He felt certain he would conquer England and wanted the castle for himself. As a result, the historic structures of Dover were never damaged in the war.

Dover Castle was Disneyland for me. The underground tunnel system and naval control centers left me speechless. I've read a half-dozen biographies of Winston Churchill, and many accounts of the terrible war years. I think Churchill saved the free world. Of course, he didn't do it by himself, but without his leadership, determination and tenacity, the world we live in today would likely be a very different place.

I was disappointed to miss Monet's Garden and Museum; but the visit to Dover Castle and Wartime Tunnels was better than anything I would likely have experienced in Giverny, France. What did that Oklahoma cowboy say? "Some of God's greatest gifts are unanswered prayers." I wasn't praying to see Monet, but visiting Dover Castle was an unexpected gift.

Dover Castle

In Flanders Fields

Monday, April 17th

In Flanders Fields, the poppies blow
Beneath the crosses, row on row.
That mark our place, and in the sky,
The larks, still bravely singing, fly
Scarce heard amid the guns below.

We are the dead, short days ago
We lived, felt dawn, saw sunset glow.
Loved and were loved, and now we
Lie,
In Flanders fields.

Take up our quarrel with the foe:
To you from failing hands we throw
The torch; be yours to hold it high.
If ye break faith with us who die
We shall not sleep, though poppies
grow
In Flanders fields.

The day before John McCrae wrote his famous poem on May 3, 1915, his close friend Lieutenant Alexis Helmer was killed in the fighting and buried in a makeshift grave amongst blooming poppies. I remember as a grade schooler we memorized this solemnly sweet poem. John

McCrae was a surgeon from Canada during World War I who served in Ypres, Belgium, and died of pneumonia on January 28, 1918, just months before the end of the war.

We visited Ypres (pronounced eepra) and toured a couple of the more than 160 military cemeteries in the area. The cemeteries are immaculately maintained by Belgians, funded by a non-profit coalition of Allied countries. Our visit was powerful, moving and humbling. At Tyne Cot Cemetery, more than 11,000 identical white marble markers covered the ground. Of the soldiers buried there, only about 30% were identified with name, rank and military unit, the remaining were simply inscribed "A Soldier of the Great War" with a cross and the words: "Known Unto God" engraved below. Some of the unknown also read, "A Canadian Soldier" or "An American Soldier" or "An Australian Soldier", etc. Those soldiers had some identification attached to a body part; the remains of the others were beyond recognition. The Tyne Cot Cemetery is located on one of many battlefields in the Ypres area. The Germans had dug trench bunkers up the hillside at Tyne Cot and armed its troops with newly invented machine guns. Allied troops stormed the hillside and were slaughtered in mass.

War is hell. Most wars are instigated by megalomaniacs like Hitler or Stalin or Putin in the insatiable pursuit of power. Or by religionist zealots, believing they have a Divine mandate to exterminate unbelievers. Our guide said that shortly after the United States entered the war, during the first hour of fighting in a single battle, 50,000 American troops were killed, and within three hours, 100,000 had lost their lives. Total insanity. The human slaughter during WWI (the Great War or the War to End All Wars) is unimaginable. History records 9 million soldiers killed, 23 million wounded and 5 million civilian deaths.

We also visited the Flanders Fields Museum in Ypres. It's an interactive museum, worthy of an all-day visit. You'd never know Ypres itself was utterly destroyed during the war. Every home, building and cathedral in the city has been built since 1918. And not just built, but re-built. Ypres looks like it dates back to the 18th-century. It's welcoming, unexpectedly historic and very charming. It's a place that evokes images of a snowy Christmas Eve by the fireside, with Santa and his elves making merry in the twinkling town square.

As if it had never been touched by the horrors of war.

Marker for a soldier "Known unto God"

Vincent

Tuesday, April 18th

Starry, starry night
Paint your palette blue and grey
Look out on a summer's day
With eyes that know the darkness in my soul

Shadows on the hills
Sketch the trees and the daffodils
Catch the breeze and the winter chills
In colors on the snowy linen land

Now, I understand, what you tried to say to me
And how you suffered for your sanity
And how you tried to set them free
They would not listen, they did not know how
Perhaps they'll listen now

Starry, starry night
Flaming flowers that brightly blaze
Swirling clouds in violet haze
Reflect in Vincent's eyes of china blue

Colors changing hue
Morning fields of amber grain

Weathered faces lined in pain
Are soothed beneath the artist's loving hand

Now, I understand, what you tried to say to me
How you suffered for your sanity
How you tried to set them free
They would not listen, they did not know how
Perhaps they'll listen now

For they could not love you
But still your love was true
And when no hope was left inside
On that starry, starry night

You took your life as lovers often do
But I could have told you, Vincent
This world was never meant for one
As beautiful as you

Starry, starry night
Portraits hung in empty halls
Frameless heads on nameless walls
With eyes that watch the world and can't forget

Like the stranger that you've met
The ragged men in ragged clothes
The silver thorn of bloody rose
Lie crushed and broken on the virgin snow

Now I think I know what you tried to say to me

How you suffered for your sanity

How you tried to set them free

They would not listen, they're not listening still

Perhaps they never will

Vincent lyrics @ Songs Of Universal Inc., Benny Bird Co. Inc.

Don McLean wrote those beautifully poignant lyrics in 1971 after reading a biography of Vincent van Gogh. Van Gogh did not pursue art until age 27, and he died ten years later on July 29, 1890. In that short time, he produced more than 800 paintings and over 1,000 drawings, plus hundreds of letters documenting his life and struggles. His father was a Protestant minister, always disappointed in his eldest son. At age 16, Vincent moved from the family home in The Hague, Netherlands, to Paris to work in his uncle's art gallery. He worked in both London and Paris galleries, but was unhappy, became difficult and withdrawn, and was fired after four years. He later became a substitute teacher, studied to be a preacher, worked in a bookstore and then moved to the mining district of Belgium to work as a lay preacher. He gave everything he possessed to the poor, ministered to the sick, preached sermons and nearly starved himself. After he was laid off as a lay preacher, he existed on a meager allowance from his parents. Depressed, he wrote imploringly to his younger brother Theo, who was at the time an art dealer. Theo suggested Vincent become an artist.

Vincent had worked in galleries and gained an appreciation for great art, but until Theo's suggestion, he had completed only a few sketches and no paintings. Notwithstanding, he seized the idea and passionately dedicated himself to art. He studied master artists and took a few art courses but was a difficult student. In his early work, he copied the masters and later began producing work which portrayed the world as he saw it. His initial work was dark and somber, but later evolved to be brilliantly colorful, energetic and unique. He was admired by fellow artists and some of his work was offered in Theo's gallery. Yet during his lifetime, he sold only one painting. Despite lack of sales, Vincent never altered his style. He had a vision of great art and pursued it relentlessly. Theo's faith in Vincent also never wavered. For years, Theo paid for Vincent's art materials and most of his living expenses. Theo and his wife Jo had a son on January 31, 1890, whom they named after Vincent. Upon that occasion Theo wrote to his brother, "...we'll name him after you, and I'm making the wish that he may be as determined and courageous as you." Upon his death, Theo had the vast majority of Vincent's paintings and drawings, but Theo unfortunately passed away six months later. Theo's 28 year old widow, Jo, and later her "determined and courageous" son, Vincent, were largely responsible for promoting the Vincent van Gogh legacy.

McLean's lyrics follow the general consensus that Vincent van Gogh committed suicide. In the last decade, new research and recent biographies have questioned that. I don't believe he committed suicide. He ordered new paint supplies the day before he was shot. On that fatal morning he was out plein air painting and encountered some young bullies who had previously harassed him. The new evidence indicates he could not have self-inflicted a wound at the angle the bullet entered his chest. The theory is that the boys may have taunted him, a gun went off and they ran. The weapon was never found. Vincent, while mortally wounded, made his way back to town and said nothing about the incident but expressed hope the bullet could be removed and he would recover. Unfortunately, there was no local surgeon, and no surgery was attempted.

We'll never know what actually happened. Yes, Van Gogh battled depression and suffered multiple nervous breakdowns, but I don't think he was suicidal at the time. His work was gaining public recognition and he was likely on the cusp of success, maybe even fame and fortune.

This Tuesday morning as I wandered the stunning Van Gogh Museum in Amsterdam, amid throngs crowding the galleries, I wondered if Vincent had a window to it all. It was difficult to get near the paintings because numerous tour groups and school field trippers, together with masses of art lovers, stood five or six deep in front of each painting. The museum was built as part of a deal negotiated by that determined nephew, Vincent. He agreed to donate his inheritance of some 205 original paintings and over 500 drawings, plus about 800 letters, mostly between Vincent and Theo, to the Vincent van Gogh Foundation, provided the Dutch state agreed to create a suitable museum in Amsterdam. The Van Gogh Museum was designed by a local architect and opened in 1973. It's a treasure. Vincent surely must be pleased and proud.

The last two lines of Don McLean's beautiful lyrics read:

They would not listen, they're not listening still,
Perhaps they never will.

On this workday Tuesday, scores of art lovers clog the galleries with museum headsets on, facing the paintings and standing five or more deep, quietly mesmerized by the man and his work. In 2022, a Christie's New York auction sold the Van Gogh painting "Orchard with Cypresses" for over $117 million dollars.

Vincent, I think they are listening. Perhaps the world *was* meant for one as beautiful as you.

Add Amsterdam

Wednesday, April 19th

There are a dozen ports to go on this voyage and I'm already being asked about my favorite cities and places. It's an evolving list, but here are the top 10 candidates so far:

Moorea, French Polynesia
Auckland, New Zealand
Tauranga, New Zealand
Sydney, Australia
Perth, Australia
Cape Town, South Africa
The Canary Islands
Marrakech, Morocco
Malaga, Spain
Lisbon, Portugal
A Coruna, Spain
Weymouth, England
Dover, England
Ypres, Belgium
Amsterdam, Netherlands

So much for that. My top 10 already includes 15, and we have 12 to go. The truth is, there are too many special places.

However, on any list, Amsterdam would make the final cut. The heart of Amsterdam beats about seven feet *below* sea level. In fact, about half of the Netherlands is below sea level. Dykes and dams surround low lying areas and windmills pump the water out to sea. Amsterdam has a system of canals that run parallel to the streets. The city is built on 11 million wooden poles, sunk deep through the clay into the bedrock. Some still-occupied buildings are actually tilting or leaning on the poles. In recent times, concrete pylons have replaced wooden poles. Uniquely, there are no skyscrapers in Amsterdam, as the pylons would not carry the weight.

Amsterdam oozes charm and openness. The politics are liberal; everyone and every non-threatening behavior is welcome and accepted. There is a famous Red Light District and almost 100 museums, including a Museum of Prostitution and an Erotic Museum. (We missed both.) And there are gazillions of bicyclists constantly ringing bells. Red paths for bicycles line every street and bikes have the absolute right of way. If a car strikes a bike, it's the car's fault, period. The bicyclist could be running a red light or riding the wrong way. It doesn't matter. And no one wears a bicycle helmet. The Dutch are big on freedom and responsibility.

Today, Amsterdam's leafy streets are lined with parked bicycles and noisy, aromatic sidewalk cafes. Long lines outside "Mannekenpis," a sidewalk takeout "Voted No. 1 Holland Fries" lured us in. The fries were thick, tender, fresh-fried, lightly salted and delicious. Served in huge paper waffle cones, we ate until we couldn't, and deposited leftovers in the bin.

Most people in Amsterdam ride bicycles, and the bikes are not exotic carbon fiber speed racers. They are simple and durable with upright handlebars, comfortable seats and a parcel rack or baby carrier on back. Young and old bike in a place where there's little demand for

Weight Watchers, despite being home to Holland's Best Fries.
Amsterdam should be on every bucket list.

Copenhagen canal

Copenhagen Beyond The Little Mermaid

Friday, April 21st

On the Copenhagen flatboat "Canal Tour," our young Danish narrator repeated each comment three times: in Danish, English and German. When we arrived at the iconic Little Mermaid statue, he said, "We are approaching the most overrated tourist attraction in Copenhagen, The Little Mermaid." It's a four foot bronze statue by Edvard Eriksen of a young topless mermaid on a modest-sized granite boulder at the water's edge. It was inspired by the 1837 fairy tale of the same name by Hans Christian Andersen. Unfortunately, it's neither imposing nor impressive. In fact, it seems silly that busloads of gawking tourists, like us, crowd around her taking grinning selfies. It's probably the least attractive attraction in Copenhagen, yet we tourists dutifully make our pilgrimage. The locals seem embarrassed by her: over the years, she has been decapitated twice, had her arm sawed off, had gallons of paint dumped over her, and been repeatedly draped in modest clothing. To discourage the vandalism, the Copenhagen City Council has considered moving her a few yards out to sea, but today she remains on the shoreline.

Earlier in the day we visited the Ny Carlsberg Glyptotek art museum. Glyptotek means "to carve," and the museum represents the private art collection of Carl Jacobsen, founder of Carlsberg Breweries. The museum features primarily ancient Greek and Roman sculpture, plus works of Danish and French impressionists including Monet, Pissarro, Renoir, Degas, Morisot and Cezanne and some post-impressionist painters including Van Gogh, Toulouse-Lautrec, Picasso, and Giacometti.

The museum also houses one of 28 cast bronze sculptures of Edgar Degas' "The Little Fourteen Year Old Dancer," which is one-third life size and was originally sculpted in wax. The original was dressed in a bodice, tutu and ballet slippers, and the various museum-owned bronze repetitions are dressed similarly. It's an evocative work: the tense pose, taut arms, interlocked hands behind her back and the facial expression all send mixed messages. Is ballet something she loves, or is she being forced to dance (or model) against her will? Degas made a career of painting ballet dancers and here he paints a psychological portrait in wax. The Little Dancer is far more interesting and intriguing than the pallid Little Mermaid.

The sun was out in Copenhagen today and so were the locals. Our ship's entertainment director has been to Copenhagen numerous times and has rarely seen a sunny day. The people crowding the sidewalks confirmed that we were enjoying the first sunny day of the season. I'm told there are 5 bicycles for every 4 people in Copenhagen, and I believe it. Copenhagen has numerous multi-level bike parking lots and relatively few car parks. We western desert dwellers take sunshine for granted, but they don't in Copenhagen. There were even a few convertible cars on the streets today, all top down. Every seat was taken in the outdoor cafes and each table carried lively conversation and laughter. There was sunshine in the soul of Denmark today.

Like Amsterdam, Copenhagen is cross-sected by canals lined by colorful 19th and early 20th-century multi-story apartment buildings and sidewalk cafes and pastry shops. It's a fabulous place for a day walk or a bike ride. Also like Amsterdam, it's charming for another reason: there's no homeless population. All around, people seemed busy, contented and happy. Hans Christian Andersen was inspired by living in this fairy tale place.

Add Copenhagen to the ever expanding list of favorites.

Vigeland Park Monolith Tower

Vigeland Sculpture Park, Oslo

Saturday, April 22nd

We spent the better part of this spring Saturday at the 110-acre Vigeland Sculpture Park in Oslo, Norway. It was another gorgeous day for winter-weary, sun-starved Scandinavians. By midmorning, Norwegians packed the park, playing lawn games, picnicking in shorts and sun-bathing in bikinis on the vast lawns. We were bundled in sweaters and windbreakers, trying to keep warm in the brisk sunshine.

The official name of the park is Frogner Park, but as Norway's most visited attraction it's generally referred to as Vigeland Park after sculptor Gustav Vigeland. There are over 200 bronze, granite and cast iron sculptures in the park, all by Vigeland. The granite Monolith Tower, at the center of the Monolith Plateau, is over 46 feet tall and comprises 121 naked human figures top to bottom. You could Google it, but you have to see it.

Gustav Vigeland was born Adolf Gustav Thorsen in southern Norway in 1869. By 1888, he had moved to Kristiania (now Oslo), determined to become a sculptor. In his 20s he and other family members adopted the surname Vigeland from the locale of his grandparent's farm. By 1894, he had traveled around Europe, studied under notable sculptors, and held his first critically acclaimed solo exhibition in Norway. In 1905, after Norway became independent from Sweden, Vigeland completed numerous public commissions for statutes and busts celebrating renowned patriots. He quickly became known as Norway's foremost sculptor, and later designed the Nobel Peace Prize medal.

As with most artists, Vigeland's work evolved over time but

maintained the primary thematic element of mortality, together with the relationship between man and woman. His early work is graphically realistic, while later works, including much of the work in Vigeland Park, are simpler and more classical. Also, in most of Vigeland's work, clothing is not optional, it's absent. The privates are rendered as realistically as the hands and feet. No need for an anatomy class in Oslo's primary schools. The entirely uninhibited Monolith Tower was sculpted from a massive granite boulder weighing several hundred tons and erected on site under a wooden shed. It took three stone carvers 14 years to transfer the 121 naked human bodies from Vigeland's plaster model to the granite. It was unveiled at Christmas, 1944, and 180,000 people passed through the wooden shed for a first look. The shed was torn down shortly thereafter.

Remarkably, in 1921, Vigeland signed a contract granting all his future work to Oslo, in exchange for the city constructing a combined studio and residence for him. The city also agreed to convert the building to a museum after his death. The resulting studio adjacent to the park is hugely impressive. Inside, he made the plaster casts for the Monolith Tower. Vigeland's prodigious output is breathtaking. Four years after his death, the city opened the museum, which contains 1,600 sculptures and 12,000 drawings, plus thousands of letters, notebooks, and photographs, along with his collection of about 5,000 books. The city must have also provided him with living expenses, as Vigeland donated his entire livelihood to the city from 1921 until his death in 1943.

The Gustav Vigeland story is so remarkable, and his life work so extensive, that touring the park and museum took most of our day. The afternoon park scene included moms pushing baby buggies, a dad teaching his boy to ride a bike, squealing kids on the slippery slide, families celebrating birthdays under balloons, young lovers whispering in the shadows and a family grilling salmon steaks. A pleasant Norwegian Saturday afternoon. It dawned on me that I hadn't seen a single smoker all day.

No wonder Norway has the fourth highest life expectancy in the world.

When we disembarked at Oslo this morning, we found two hop-on-hop-off bus companies waiting dockside. Both companies had similar pricing and routes. I asked Nyron, our HAL excursions director if he had a recommendation. He said they were both good but pointed to the one on the right as "sponsored by Holland America." We boarded that one. As we approached Vigeland Park, the driver said a marathon was being run in the city, which required street closure at the regular bus stop. Accordingly, he changed routes and dropped us mid-block at a side entrance to Vigeland Park. I took a photo of the drop location, and the driver said the last bus would arrive at 4:30 pm.

We returned to the drop off point at 3:45 pm. No one was there, but I was confident we had arrived at the designated spot in plenty of time. Christeen said she wanted to grab a Pepsi in an enclosed mall up the street. I told her to be quick about it, as she is easily distracted in a shopping environment. A few minutes later, another couple arrived and said the pick up location was changed to the other side of the street. I crossed the street, and 10 minutes later, the bus arrived. Fearing it was the last bus of the day, I asked the driver to wait a moment while I searched for Christeen. He mumbled something about being on schedule. I race-clopped to the mall, and finally found Christeen in a basement store, blithely browsing blouses. We scurried up the escalator to the street and found the bus had departed. We waited another 25 minutes and were about to hire a taxi when the last bus arrived.

Late afternoon traffic was heavy and streets were still closed for race stragglers. Our driver made repeated detours to avoid the closures, but ultimately got stuck on a narrow street with no turn-around option. After about 5 minutes, the driver got off the bus and walked away. I thought maybe he'd gotten off to make a call, but he didn't return. After another 10 minutes, fellow passengers began to panic. We were on the upper deck and could hear the comments from passengers below.

"Where did the driver go?"

"How rude is that?"

"Maybe he just quit. And left us stranded!"

"Did he leave the keys in the ignition?"

"Does anyone know how to drive a bus?"

"Does anyone have cell service? Can you call the bus company?"

"I tried to call and the office is closed. It goes to voicemail!"

"We'll never get back to the ship in time and Holland America will leave us!!"

Meanwhile, racers were still periodically passing along the closed street. The panicky chatter continued and the volume ascended. Finally, I'd heard enough and took the stairs below.

"People. People!" I said."Relax. This is a HAL-sponsored bus and the ship will not leave us."

They finally quieted and presently the driver returned. Upon questioning, he said he'd gone to the next stop to say he'd pick them up after the street reopened.

Such a nice guy.

Blustery, Artsy Kristiansand

Sunday, April 23rd

On this blustery, rainy Norwegian morning an *enclosed* double decker hop-on- hop-off bus sat at the dock. We quickly bought tickets and waited for our friends who were paying with Norwegian kroner. When the attendant couldn't print tickets with a cash payment, I offered my credit card to our cardless friends. (Remember the Cape Town credit card caper?) As the attendant ran my card again, the warm, fully enclosed bus drove away.

We annoyedly zipped up and waited until the next bus, with an open top and cold, wet seats, arrived 30 minutes later. The route from the harbor included a bitterly blustery ride on the freeway to the Kristiansand Zoo and Amusement Park. Being Sunday, it was closed. The bus promptly made a u-turn and 20 freezing minutes later we were back in the historic town center.

We happily hopped off that rolling Frigidare at the circa 1885 Kristiansand Cathedral. A Lutheran cathedral, it was historically a part of the Church of Norway. The Norwegian government and church were tied until 2017, when the church became a private legal entity. We entered the cathedral just as Sunday services ended and were greeted by a kindly young pastor. She confirmed that Norway is overwhelmingly Lutheran; however, member attendance these days is generally limited to holidays and events: Christmas, Easter, baptisms, weddings and funerals. On a given Sunday, the 1,000 seat cathedral might have 100 to 150 worshipers. The cathedral was imposing and impressive outside, but rather modest inside. No glittering gold, no ornate statues, no lavish paintings or art. The building had a warm, inviting feel to it. Like a church.

Rain had been forecast all day, but by early afternoon, the sun appeared and warmed the relentless bluster. We strolled along the harbor, past the closed historic Kristiansand Fortress. In Norway, most businesses, monuments and museums are closed Sundays. As a result, the old-town Kristiansand was reverently quiet all afternoon.

Quiet helps us see things we may otherwise miss. In Norway, manhole covers are etched with unique community designs. The Kristiansand cover is engraved with an image of the cathedral, plus two additional historic buildings and "Kristiansand 1641" across the top. It's a lovely work of art. But Norway doesn't have a lock on artistic manhole covers. The manholes in our hometown of St. George, Utah, are beautifully engraved with the morning sun rising over the mountainous desert landscape.

Interestingly, some people actually collect manhole art. That requires plenty of sturdy storage space, a strong back and a ready supply of Odor Eaters.

Pastor at Kristiansand Cathedral

Haugesund Me Home

Monday, April 24th

The village of Haugesund, Norway, at the end of the protective waters of the Karmsund Strait on the N0rth Sea coast, is postcard-pretty. We arrived on a chilly, wet and windswept Monday morning. Haugesund was once known for herring fishing and processing. Today the herring population has been depleted and the local economy, like much of Norway, is primarily dependent on North Sea oil.

I was disappointed that the local art museum was closed but delighted by the bookstores and toy shops in town. By midmorning, the sun appeared and transformed Haugesund village into a sunny Santa's Workshop. I half expected to see the jolly old man and his elves walking along the cobblestone walkway. "Haraldsgate" is a dozen blocks long and lined by children's book and toy shops with colorfully happy storefronts. Funky grandma and grandpa shops galore. In most stores, the books were printed in Norwegian, but we happened upon one kiddie shop with an upstairs loft entirely devoted to classic English literature and toy cars. Christeen had to lasso me out of that one.

Famished by protracted book and toy shopping, we lunched at a pastry shop on tuna and avocado-tomato sandwiches. Plus custard-filled chocolate donuts. Several dining tables featured fresh donuts under a glass top. Brilliant idea. Could anyone eat odiferous tuna over luscious creamy donuts without yielding? (Reminds me of that famous Oscar Wilde quote: "I can resist everything except temptation.") And if that weren't enough, the rear wall was covered with fresh hanging frosted donuts. Ripe for the picking. How about a dozen to go?

Take me back to Haugesund.

Eidfjord Fantasy

Tuesday, April 25th

Eidfjord is a tiny shoreline hamlet of a few hundred souls with a deep water dock at the end of the Eid Fjord. Dockside, the gigantic Zuiderdam dwarfs the little town. Eid Fjord is an inner branch of the winding, 111-mile-long Hardangerfjorden. Fjords are u-shaped canyons carved by melting glaciers moving toward the open sea. Over time, ancient receding glaciers have carved many miles of deep oceanic canyons, enabling massive cruise ship access to tiny remote shoreline villages. The scenery along the Norway fjords is camera clicking nirvana.

Charming, touristy Eidfjord is characterized by modest hotels, bed and breakfasts, campgrounds and souvenir shops. It's a favorite resort destination for the big city dwellers in Oslo and Bergen. The nearby attractions include the scenic fjords, the Hardangervidda mountain glacier and Voringfossen waterfall.

We rented a car with two other couples and drove to the Hardangervidda Plateau and the famous waterfalls. Enroute, we drove through multiple short and long mountain tunnels. Atop the plateau, we encountered heavy, wet snowfall and 5 to 10-foot plowed snow banks along the road. We stopped at a quaint roadside lodge for hot chocolate and "the first homemade carrot cake of the season." For arctic camping adventurers, an octagonal canvas tent was tethered to an imposing snow bank behind the lodge.

Having neither time nor interest in glacial tent camping, we drove to Voringsfossen waterfall. From our dramatic canyon-top viewpoint, the plunging 600- foot vertical-drop waterfall visually and aurally exploded down the canyon wall to the icy riverbed. Splendid stainless-steel stairs and decks over the canyon walls provided panoramic views on both sides of the canyon. The majesty of Voringsfossen reminded me of Yellowstone Falls, except the drop at Yellowstone is only about 300 feet and the view toward the falls is considerably less stimulating than standing atop a 600-foot crashing waterfall.

Halfway down the mountain, we stopped at the spectacular new Norsk Natursenter (Nature Center), a "modern experience center for Norwegian nature, climate and environment." It's a gem, with multiple interactive displays, stocked aquariums and life-sized plant, bird, fish and animal renderings. The best part is a new 20-minute feature film called "Fjord, Mountains and Waterfalls." Spectacularly filmed by helicopter and drone, with a gigantic 180 degree wraparound screen and soaring soundtrack, it may be the best nature film ever. If I only had a wrap-around television.

Upon returning to Eidfjord, we couldn't resist a scenic drive along the fabulously winding fjord-front roadway. When dry, Norway roads are motorbike and sportscar paradise. No potholes, perpetual sensuous curves and precious little traffic.

On my next Norway adventure, please toss the extra undies and pack me a bullet bike.

Ron, Kyle and Charles

Christeen at Hardangervidda Plateau

Clothing the Needy

Thursday, April 27th

I have no excuse; I've done multi-week motorcycle trips and I know about packing light. Still, I overpacked for this cruise. When we crossed the equator the second time, I was ready to chuck all my extra hot-weather, and otherwise unnecessary shoes, pants, shorts and shirts. Plus, I need room for more books. I tried to give some clothes to our cabin stewards, but my clothes are too big. Then last week HAL announced a two-hour "Orange Elephant Day" sale (aka white elephant), allowing passengers to load tables poolside on the Lido deck with unwanted stuff for sale. Anything unsold would be disposed of by the HAL "standard company recycling." Whatever that means. I didn't want to sell anything but was delighted to dispose of a bag of unnecessary clothes. At the appointed hour, I laid the following on a vacant table, avoiding eye contact with the milling crowd:

1 pair walking shoes

2 pair swim trunks

1 pair walking shorts

6 t-shirts

5 golf shirts

3 pair pants

As I turned away, a lady grabbed a pair of pants, searching for the size and asked, "How much?" I replied, "Nothing, take them." An hour and a half later, confident that all my stuff would be sent to the HAL recycling bin, I walked past my table. It was empty, but for a pair of swim trunks. My needy fellow world cruisers had taken all.

Is there anything more gratifying than clothing the needy?

Weathering Bergen

Wednesday, April 26th

We arrived in Bergen on a crisp, sunny spring morning. Patrick, our local guide, immediately apologized for the weather, "Sunshine is entirely out of character here," he quipped. Patrick spoke perfect midwestern English and later confessed he grew up in Chicago and followed his wife (as extra baggage) to Bergen. Two years ago, she took a job as an important person at a local art museum.

Bergen was founded in 1070, and by the 13th-century, it was the capital and largest city of Norway, later ceding those distinctions to Oslo. Patrick said it currently has a population of around 300,000 and assured us it remains "the superior city." Bergen lies just above the 60th parallel (similar to Anchorage, AK) and enjoys a rather mild climate, thanks to prevailing wind currents originating in the Gulf of Mexico. The record Bergen high temperature is 92 degrees Fahrenheit, and the record low is 2 degrees. By contrast, our summer cabin near Mackay, Idaho, which is hundreds of miles south at about the 45th parallel, has a record high of 100 degrees and a record low of 40 below zero. Bergen also enjoys bountiful rain from the Gulf Stream. It's the rainiest city in Europe, averaging around 239 rainy days a year with nearly 100 inches of annual rainfall.

Patrick narrated our dramatic day-long tour (which included ferrying the bus across Fuja fjord) around Hardanger fjord and other fjord forks. Not surprisingly, the most dramatic feature of our Bergen area tour was the weather. There's a saying in Norway, "There's no such thing as bad weather, only bad clothes." After leaving the dock, and before we reached the opposite side of the city, it was already overcast. Then it started raining. Later, partly sunny. Then more rain. Then hail. Then snow. Then it was cloudy and rainy. Then it was sunny. Then hail again. Repeated all day long. We entered one long mountain tunnel in a fierce, windy hailstorm and exited a few miles later to a beautiful sunny day, the road bare and dry. I've never seen such weather.

In the countryside, we visited a small wooden church dating to 1306, which burned centuries later and was rebuilt in 1726. The church sits off the road below a sloping vacant parcel accessible only by a descending dirt pathway. In order to help preserve the ancient church, we were told services are held only once a year. Curiously however, a gazillion tourists trek into it each year. We were welcomed into the building by a Norwegian guide who asked us to be seated with the women on the left side and the men on the right. (Certain other places of worship require similar separation seating). She explained the church faces east towards the rising sun, following the theory that evil comes from the left (or the cold north). The women are accordingly seated on the left to protect the men from evil. For which we men are grateful.

Snow tires are required by law in Norway. It snows in Bergen, but usually melts quickly. Nearby, higher elevations receive lots of snow, and it sticks. A driver's license is a prized possession here. According to Patrick, a license requires mandatory driver education in all driving conditions, including nighttime and rain and snow. Between license fees and fees for mandatory classes, a driver's license can cost upwards of $3,000. Public transit in and around the big cities is good, so one can get by without a driver's license, and many do. Patrick also mentioned there is virtually no drunk driving problem in Norway, since the minimum blood alcohol level for conviction is a very low .02%. (In California it's .08%.) And if you are caught drunk driving, you lose your license.

Of all the places I've seen on this cruise, Norway is the winner. The natural landscape is breathtakingly beautiful. The people are healthy, happy, hard-working, self-reliant and friendly. The standard of living is excellent, thanks to oil revenues from offshore drilling rigs. Most Norwegian families own a home, and many have vacation homes in the mountains or along the coast. Most medical care and college tuition is free. The liberals love to point to Norway as a shining example of effective social liberalism. But they never mention that before the discovery of black gold in the North Atlantic, Norway was dirt poor. And no liberal seems to consider what happens to Norway if the world achieves carbon neutrality and the North Atlantic oil wells are capped. Windmills and solar panels will never fund Norwegian free medical care and college tuition. At least rainy Norway should always have economical and environmentally friendly hydroelectric power.

I believe we're a long way from weaning ourselves off fossil fuels. Unless and until that happens, Norway is one of the best places in the world to live. If you don't believe me, ask any Norwegian. And if you're lucky enough to spend time in Norway, bring a good coat.

Fjord boathouse

Skye Island Caveat Emptor

Friday, April 28th

We are docked at Portree, the tiny capital of the Isle of Skye off the northwest coast of Scotland. I feel appreciated here. The name Kyle appears repeatedly in Scotland, on road and street signs and on maps. "Kyle" is Scottish for a strait between an island and the mainland or between two islands. My local map identifies multiple Kyles: Kyle More, Kyle Rona, Kyle Rhea, Kyle Scalpay and numerous Kyle streets and roads. There is even a village, Kyle of Lochalsh. There's probably a monument somewhere as well, but we missed it.

Christeen believes one Kyle is plenty, so we struck out for Dunvegan Castle and Gardens. The castle was originally built in the 13th-century, with a tower added in the 14th and subsequent modifications and expansions until about 1840. It's always been the historic seat of the Clan of MacLeod and sits on a rock about 50 feet above the sea, facing an inlet. In the 20th-century the Clan modernized the castle interior with plumbing, electrical, and smooth wallboard surfacing over the stone walls and ceilings. Outside, it's a stately and formidable stone-towered castle perched atop a rock. Inside it's cool, high ceilinged, drafty and cluttered with historic "clan chief" portraits and family heirlooms dating through the centuries. Unfortunately, we had half the time needed in the castle and no time for the picturesque grounds and multiple gardens descending toward the sea.

During the long ride back to the ship, the rolling and greening Scottish countryside was like a movie reel. Sheep outnumber people in Scotland by over a million. Along the countryside, flocks of sheep grazed within fenced plots. Shearing season must be near, as the sheep looked like mini wooly mammoths. Except for all the little lambies, which playfully bounced around like puppies. "Mary had a little lamb, a little lamb, a little lamb; Mary had a little lamb with fleece as white as snow." I couldn't get that annoying jingle out of my head.

We returned to pretty Portree village and searched the seaside shops for genuine Scottish woolens. We entered a quaint "Knit Shop," and Christeen found a handsome men's v-neck wool sweater at a good price. The tag carried a genuine Scottish brand, but the wool seemed a bit thin. I searched for the consumer tag sewn to the inside seam. It read "100% Wool" and "Made in Bangladesh."

Caveat Emptor. Even in quaint Portree, Scotland.

Dunvegan Castle

Magnificent Inveraray Castle

Saturday, April 29th

It took an hour by bus from the western port in Oban over the greening Scottish Highlands to reach Inveraray Castle. If Dunvegan Castle were the Idaho State Capitol, then Inveraray Castle would be the White House. Inveraray has been the seat of the Dukes of Argyll, chiefs of the Clan Campbell, since it was laid out in 1743 by Archibald Campbell, soon to become the 3rd Duke of Argyll. The castle replaced a 15th-century castle on the same site. It is surrounded by a 16-acre garden and is part of a 60,000-acre estate. Argyll is a county in western Scotland and the Duke is the highest rank of peerage (nobility). Scottish peerage in descending order of rank is duke, marquess, earl, viscount and baron.

The current, or 13th, Duke of Argyll, Torquhil Campbell (born 1968), grew up in the castle and his wife, Eleanor Cadbury (of the Cadbury chocolate family), and their three children occupy two of the upper floors. The Duke is the captain of Scotland's national elephant polo team, which won the World Elephant Polo Championships in 2004 and 2005. (And I thought pony polo was an expensive sport.) The Duke's championship elephant polo jersey is on display inside the castle in a glass case. Also on display are over 1,300 pikes (long spears), muskets and swords, together with an unbelievable amount of priceless clan artifacts.

I could have spent hours at Inveraray Castle. Part of the 2012 Christmas episode of Downton Abbey was filmed here. We never made it to the glorious gardens. Our daughters would have been absolutely gob-smacked over the place. Every room, every artifact, every piece of furniture and every painting was a treasure. I took a few pictures, realizing my photos would never capture the majesty.

In the gift shop, I bought a picture book titled *Inveraray Castle and Gardens*, with the cover autographed by the Duke himself. The friendly cashier gave me a receipt, then handed the book to the 13th Duke of Argyll, who bagged it and thanked me for visiting his "home."

I should've got an autographed elephant polo jersey.

Inveraray Castle

Dearest Dublin, I Want More

Sunday, April 30th

We tendered in light rain across choppy seas from the ship to a pedestrian pontoon dock at Dun Laoghaire (pronounced Dun Leery). We were greeted by a couple of crazy Irishmen who teasingly directed us to the train running from Dun Laoghaire to Dublin. After a brisk 30-minute rail commute, we disembarked the train in midtown Dublin and boarded a tour bus opposite the train station. The two-hour, superbly narrated tour covered most of the important sights in this Irish capital of around 1.3 million people in the metro area. Our tour included the famous Guinness & Co. Brewery at St. James Gate. The Irish love Guinness and whiskey. The original four acre site was leased in 1759 to Arthur Guinness at 45 English pounds per year for *9,000 years*. That's not a typo. The company subsequently bought the property, (why?) and over the years, dramatically expanded the site and operations. Our narrator said at one time there were over 10,000 employees at the brewery. Today, thanks to automation, that number is around 800. It's estimated that 10 million glasses of Guinness per day are consumed worldwide. That equates to 1.8 *billion* pints a year. I didn't think we drank that much water. By the end of the tour we were slathered in Guinness history and needed a pint.

We wandered around O'Connell Street and happened upon Murray's Public House. The first pub was opened on the Murray's site in 1797. Many proprietors and different businesses occupied the building until a fruit purveyor and florist, Miss Alicia Lambe acquired it in the late 1890s. Her business was referenced in James Joyce's novel *Ulysses*. Today, Murray's is a traditional Irish pub, with bottles of Irish whiskey lining dark varnished walls, brassy ceilings and non-traditional big screen

TVs. I found a slice of heaven in Murray's: a superb BLT sandwich with fries and an iced Coke Zero under a muted live Formula One TV broadcast from Azerbaijan. And from overhead speakers, Led Zeppelin, Creedence, the Yardbirds, the Beatles and various Irish folk rockers streaming sweet rock n' roll. Whiskey-free heaven.

After lunch, we reviewed the 68 attractions highlighted on our Dublin city map and made a short list: National Gallery of Ireland, Dublin Castle, Christ Church Cathedral, St. Patrick's Cathedral, Irish Rock n' Roll Museum, Museum of Irish Literature, Dublin Writers Museum and the James Joyce Center. Time constraints and train schedules limited us to Christ Church Cathedral, which was ghastly ornate and embarrassingly gaudy. I can't understand how the church in those days justified such excess in the name of the Father, the Son and the Holy Spirit. It's like there could never be enough gilding, glazing, painting, sculpting, and casting. But what a time to be an artist.

After returning to ship, we were entertained by the "Irish Folk Music and Dancers" on the World Stage. The Dublin group consisted of an accordion player, a guitarist and an Irish "bodhran" drummer, plus four dancers. All were terrific, with the dancers clicking, clacking and sashaying across the stage. The drummer sang a tearful Irish ballad about a poor bugger who "spent near all 'is money on whiskey and Guinness, then wasted the rest of it."

When he heard our next port was Cork, he shook his head. "Feelin' sorry fer ya," he said. "Thems Corkers is a backward lot. Ya hears 'em speakin' but ya won't get a word of it till yur round 'em fer a bit. Then ya realize thur speakin' Inglish after all."

Sadly, we had no time to get a satisfying taste of Dublin. I've been wanting to visit Dublin, the setting of *Ulysses* by James Joyce, for years. For many literary scholars, *Ulysses* is the greatest English novel ever written. I don't know about that, but James Joyce was gifted and enigmatic. The novel is dense and difficult, littered with puns, metaphors, parodies and allusions. Its 783 pages follow the itinerant Leopold Bloom in Dublin for just one day, June 16, 1904. The date was not randomly picked; it's the date of Joyce's first sexual encounter with his future wife, Nora Barnacle. Upon publication in 1922, the novel was immediately banned as obscene in the US and UK, and was not even openly available in Ireland until the 1960s. Now June 16th, or "Bloomsday" is observed annually in Dublin and elsewhere, celebrating the life of James Joyce. The novel's primary characters reference Homer's epic poem *The Odyssey.* The prose imitates many writing styles and seems confusing, chaotic and disorganized, with no chapter divisions, headings or titles. Sections of the book are written in the style of a traditional novel, others as a Shakespearean play, and the last 50 pages are a single sentence with almost no punctuation. I tried to read it years ago and gave up. It can't be read recreationally. It must be read slowly and deliberately. Before tackling it on this cruise, I read Homer's *Odyssey*, and all the Shakespearean sonnets, plus *Hamlet*. To get through it, I read it not as chapters in a novel, but as individual paragraphs or even sentences. The prose is alternately difficult, disgusting, funny, obtuse, revolting and brilliant. Reading it once invites you to do it again. In a weird way, like reading scripture. Similar to a one-day visit in a fabulous city. It invites you to come back again.

A taste of Dublin begs for a deep immersion.

Annie Moore and brothers

From Cobh to Cork

Monday, May 1st

      Cobh (pronounced Cove), home of Ireland's only dedicated cruise ship terminal, is a small seaside hamlet (population around 15,000). It lies on the sloping south coast of Ireland and has the dubious distinction of being the final port of call for the Titanic before she crossed the Atlantic on her ill-fated maiden voyage. It is also distinguished by the Cobh Old Church Museum, which memorializes the World War I torpedoing, on May 7, 1915, of the passenger liner RMS Lusitania by a German U-boat. Of the 1959 Lusitania passengers and crew, 1198 perished. Over 100 were buried in the adjacent Old Church Cemetery.

      Cobh was also the departure point for 2.5 million of the 6 million Irish immigrants to North America between 1848 and 1950. On January 1, 1892, young Annie Moore from Cobh was the first person to pass through the new Ellis Island Immigration Center in New York. A charming statue of Annie and her younger brothers graces the dock in Cobh.

      Cobh was also the departure point for our train to Cork. The singing drummer on the World Stage last night was correct: at first glance Cork seemed a bit seedy and backward compared to Dublin and Dun Laoghaire. But after the mile walk from the railyard to town, we found ourselves immersed once again in friendly Irish charm at Cork.

      The first Monday in May is Labour Day in Ireland. Consequently, Cork was mostly asleep until about noon, then the stores, shops and museums opened and the slumbering city awakened. We visited the lovely circa 1724 Customs House, which is now Crawford Art Gallery, Cork's "most visited cultural attraction." It was a dud. Lovely building, great provenance and a good, but limited, exhibition of sculpture (we've been spoiled by Vigeland in Oslo). Unfortunately, most of the museum's permanent collection was not on display, and only one painting captured me. There were several closed galleries and the open galleries held current exhibitions of mostly contemporary crap. We did enjoy the friendly free admission.

We hiked across the Lee river, uphill to the ancient Cathedral of St. Mary and St. Anne. It was not a dud. Construction began on the massive neo-Gothic cathedral in 1799 and it was dedicated in 1808. It had been renovated over ensuing generations, but beginning in 1965, the cathedral was extended, towers added, and the interior was stripped and simplified. Another major renovation between 1994 and 1996 included installation of fabulous abstract stained glass windows behind the altar and along the cathedral walls. The cathedral is now refreshingly light, airy, inviting and truly magnificent, without being ostentatious. Very atypical of historic Catholic cathedrals.

We returned to Cobh in time to visit the Cathedral Church of St. Colman, or simply, Cobh Cathedral. This one is typically and ghastly ostentatious. Construction began in 1867, with an initial budget of 25,000 pounds. When it was completed 52 years later in 1919, it had cost almost 10 times the original budget, making it the most expensive building ever built in Ireland up to that time. It sits on a rock hillside above the town and its 300 foot steeple also makes it the tallest church in Ireland. It absolutely dwarfs Cobh — like sticking a granite Zuiderdam on a hill above Park City, UT, and adding a 300-foot smokestack. But the massive over-the-top exterior is pedestrian compared to the embarrassingly glitzy interior. It's ridiculously overdone.

That said, both Christeen and I love the stunning exterior and interior architecture and design of historic cathedrals. They are treasuries of fine art through the ages. Give credit to the Catholic church for blessing the world with architects, stained glass craftsmen, stone, metal and wood sculptors and the world's greatest master painters. But for the church, most artists from Medieval Times through the Middle Ages and the Renaissance would never have become artists. They couldn't have made a living at it. In most historic cities, the best museums are the cathedrals. And most are open to the public free of charge or at nominal fee. Even if they are profoundly pretentious and absurdly over-decorated, we love visiting them.

During the sail away, we were once again serenaded by a local brass band. Christeen and I stood on our stateroom balcony and applauded and waved as the band played 60s and 70s rock n' roll hits. As the ship left the wharf, the band struck up the United States Navy theme, "Anchors Aweigh." People were lined all along the harbor, outside shops and in outdoor cafes, waving and cheering. People we met in Cobh couldn't believe we'd been on this ship for over four months.

Tonight, these lovely people made me feel like the luckiest guy in the world.

Ponta Delgada, Sao Miguel, Azores

Thursday, May 4th

With only two ports remaining, both in the Azores, we'll soon make a 6 sea day run to Ft. Lauderdale. Ponta Delgada is the capital of the Azores, a volcanic island region of Portugal. The Azores were a historic navigational waypoint, as winds around the islands helped push sailing vessels to the Mediterranean. I've seen travel videos of the Azores, but Ponta Delgada looks nothing like I expected. It is black and white urbanity. I expected a lush green island similar to Polynesia. In fairness, we didn't leave the city today, so we missed the countryside. Tomorrow, we'll hire a car in Praia Da Vitoria and find some lush and green.

Ponta Delgada is a community of around 70,000 and appears black and white because of the basalt (volcanic black lava rock) used on buildings and in the streets. The narrow streets and sidewalks are paved with basalt, with decorative highlights in white limestone imported from Portugal. Most buildings are white stucco with basalt on foundations and in window and corner treatments. The climate here is mild due to Gulf Stream effects. In Ponta Delgada the temperature typically varies from 55 to 77 degrees Fahrenheit, and it's regularly overcast or rainy. We enjoyed one of the rainy days.

With two other couples, we hired a horse-drawn carriage for a city tour. Joseph, our guide, was dressed like Charles Dickens in a top hat, and his Cinderella carriage was drawn by a pair of white horses. We clippity-clopped around town for an hour, with horse bells jingling as if mounted on Christmas clydesdales. Christeen loved it; I curmudgeonly endured the totally touristy cheese with a determinedly happy face.

After the cloppity buggy ride, we asked Joseph for his favorite lunch spot. He directed us in the drizzle to a modest side street cafe. The menu was entirely in Portuguese and included a special lunch buffet. The helpful waitress escorted me to the buffet table with metal warming trays loaded with something resembling animal fodder. She pointed to each tray in succession and said, "Pork. Fish. Meat. Beans." I winced and selected the beans. That was four hours ago. So far so good.

After walking in light rain all afternoon, we chanced upon the Carlos Machado Museum of religious art. The building looked odd, a basalt and white stucco museum attached to a circa 1592 Jesuit convent and church. Because it appeared odd and because it was raining and we were tired, we debated entering. The museum charged a paltry one euro entrance fee. We've seen many cathedrals cluttered with religious art, so I thought this visit would be a quickie. We entered, passed through a hallway with religious paintings, and then I caught my breath. Inside the old Jesuit church, extensive and intricate wood carvings surrounded the altar and covered the soaring ceilings and all the panels under a dozen archways. Beyond that, numerous impossibly intricate, finely detailed wooden statucs lincd cvcry wall. It would've taken sculptors and artisans decades, maybe generations, to complete the woodwork inside that massive church. The pictures I took are a joke; they convey nothing. A quick visit? Forget it. My head's still spinning.

It's a Wrap: Praia da Vitória, Terceira

Cinco de Mayo: Friday, May 5th

This is it, the last port of call for the Holland America World Cruise 2023. It's been a wonderful experience in all respects. I am ready to be home and hug my beautiful family, kiss all the babies and slog into the deferred detritus awaiting. But this evening as we watched the beautiful Terceira Island recede in the distance, I felt some sail-away sadness.

Praia da Vitória (Beach of Victory) is a romantic seaside hamlet of maybe 25,000. We hired a car and driver and toured the entire island. Indeed, Terceira is lushly green, cleverly disguising the fact that it's an active volcanic island. We asked our driver Paulo to certify our island tour would be eruption free. He looked at us like we were whackos from Utah. Legal parcels on the island are defined by basalt fences. Early settlers cleared the land by gathering and stacking the basalt rocks, which at the time, covered the entire island. Today, sturdy black and white holstein milk cows graze lazily on abundant lush grass within the fenced parcels, giving the island a relaxed, rural feel.

We drove to the oldest city in the Azores, Angra do Heroismo (Bay of Heroes), founded in 1478 and designated as a World Heritage site by UNESCO in 1983. Off the Old Angra Square, we visited a circa 1500s church with remnants of fading original frescos still visible on some of the interior walls. We toured several historic forts, battlements, churches and convents on the ruggedly picturesque island.

We also visited the volcanic wonder of the Azores; the Algar do Carvo (Cavern of Coal). The term "coal" is a misnomer, as there is no coal in the cavern, only black basalt and multi-colored shale. The cavern is a 300-foot-deep ancient lava tube, or hole in the ground, courtesy of an extinct volcano. The descent is steep and slippery, with water dripping from stalactite-lined rock walls and ceilings into a black pond at the bottom. We slid down the moss-covered steps, took photos at the pond and prayed the ancient volcano would not begin puking lava on our way up.

We milked poor Paulo for every possible minute and mile of our last tour at our final port. The "all-aboard" time was a non-negotiable 4:30 pm, and we arrived just slightly later to the stifled scowls of the otherwise accommodating ship's staff. They stored the gangway as soon as we ascended, and the Zuiderdam cast off for Ft. Lauderdale.

Six sweet sea days ahead, then back to the real world.

Praia da Vitoria

Reflections

Sunday, May 7th

Would I do it again? Absolutely, yes. It was incredible. A geographical, historical, geological, cultural, religious, political, dialectic, oceanic, biological, musical, culinary, botanical, artistic and navigational class/lesson/course/experience on steroids. I loved it all. World cruising is an immersive educational experience. Like anything else, you get what you put into it, but having access to so much in so little time has been remarkable.

On the other hand, four-and-a-half months is a long time to be away from loved ones and snow shoveling. In case we couldn't get enough, I also made a refundable deposit last year on the 2024 world cruise with an entirely different itinerary: south to the Amazon River then to Japan, China, Asia, the Middle East, Mediterranean and Europe. Much of that we've not seen, so the itinerary was attractive. But two world cruises back-to-back in two years is a bit much. I plan to transfer that refundable deposit to the 2025 "Pole to Pole" world cruise, which is on a smaller ship, sailing from Florida around South America, including cruising Antarctica and the Amazon River before returning to Europe, then on to Iceland, Greenland and Newfoundland.

The 2025 is a tad longer, at 133 days, but it departs later, at the end of January, and returns in the first week of June. The deposit is refundable, so no worries, unless Holland America goes bankrupt, and if it does, that's life.

There are some folks on ship in their late 80s and early 90s who've been on many world cruises; some have lost a spouse and don't want to exit life in a retirement home. A friend speculated that five or more have passed away during this cruise; that has to be expected, given that maybe 50% of the 1,400 passengers are in their late 70s or older. Not a bad way to go, actually. Most of the couple dozen friends we've been hanging out with are near our age and in our situation, with a bunch of kids and grandkids at home. However, there are many couples around our age that are in "thank you, next" marriages with dysfunctional kids or few kids or no kids. For them, long-term retirement cruising is a no brainer. I don't see us doing this repeatedly, but cruising is an easy, relaxing and fun way to see the world in a very short time.

World cruising also changes your perspective. Instead of just being a citizen of a city, or state, region or country, you begin to become a citizen of the world. You more profoundly appreciate the majesty and diversity of God's creation of this planet and everything on and in it. Yes, we can watch wonderful BBC documentaries like *Our Planet*, but believe me, it's not the same. Suddenly places you've never heard of, like Reunion Island and Nuku Hiva, are real. You know where they are, you've walked the streets, you've eaten the food and you've talked to the people. If the local news reports political unrest or a drought in Namibia, it's not just some obscure spot. You know where it is and what it looks like. You've been there. It's an experience few will ever have, unmatched by any other.

When we're home, we'll have to re-adjust to preparing meals, grocery shopping, doing laundry, bed making, toilet cleaning and paying for entertainment. This cruise has been a short-term escape from some personal responsibilities, combined with a healthy dose of world reality. As with anything, there are folks on board who complain, and while nothing is perfect, there's nothing worth complaining about. It's been a fabulous experience. I'm thankful to have done it and look forward to doing it again.

Acknowledgements

I'm especially grateful to my patient and loving daughter, Mindi Bullick for her careful reading of the manuscript and her numerous suggestions for correcting my pathetic punctuation, clunky phrasing, and superfluous wordiness. Without her gentle saber, you dear reader, would still be slogging through it.

And thanks to the many friends who followed my blog throughout the cruise and made helpful and encouraging comments and suggestions along the way.

Finally, thanks to Christeen, for setting aside her concerns and willingly taking the plunge on a world cruise. For also reading the manuscript and making helpful suggestions. For her unwavering support in whatever I chose to do. Mostly, for nurturing our five beautiful daughters and their wonderful families. She is and always has been an incalculable blessing in my life.